WILLIAM FRANCIS STURNER

AENEAS

THE BIOGRAPHY OF A SOUL

Dedicated

To Joyce Scozza Libutti

A Trusted Friend and Dear Cousin
Film Maker Par Excellence
Knows the Heights and the Depths
Lives Spiritually in the Moment
Dual Citizenship in Heaven and the Here-and-Now
Already Has One Foot on Earth II
The Other to Follow as She Desires
Ever Joyful, Witty, Fierce and Loving

Other Books by William Francis Sturner

BIOGRAPHICAL

Love Loops: A Divorced Father's Personal Journey (1983)

CREATIVITY

AHA: Creating Each Day with Insight and Daring (2000)

LEADERSHIP AND ORGANIZATIONAL CHANGE

Action Planning (1974)
Impact: Transforming Your Organization (1993)
Superb Leadership: The 12 Essential Skills (1997)

MYTHIC SPIRIT TALES

The Three-Legged Deer: Exploring the Miracles of Nature (2010)
Kindred Spirits: Celebrating Angels, Mystics and Miracles (2011)

THE PSYCHOLOGY OF RISK AND CHANGE

Calculated Risk: Strategies for Managing Change (1990)
Risking Change: Ending and Beginnings (1987)

SPIRITUAL COMMENTARY

Mystic in the Marketplace: A Spiritual Journey (1994)
The Creative Impulse: Celebrating Adam and Eve, Jung and EveryOne (1998)
Trust Your Immortal Soul: A Guide to Spiritual Living (2012 & 2016)
Yeshua: The Continuing Presence of the Master Soul (2017)
The Return: Traveling with Mother Mary (2022)

Contents

AENEAS

THE BIOGRAPHY OF A SOUL

Introduction

The Essential Perspective

Eternal Trinity

EACH OF US IS CONSTANTLY INVOLVED IN THE PROCESS OF CRE-ATING AN EPIC DRAMA, A STORY THAT AFFIRMS WHO WE REALLY are. In doing so, we uncover and celebrate the three major aspects of our identity.

We are a unique combination, an amalgam of three interwoven parts: an interactive human being, an immortal Soul, and a facet of divinity.

The most apparent aspect is the everyday *Me* - the embodied human being who eats, works and pursues my everyday interests. This is the personal physical part of my everyday personality.

Then there is the innermost portion of My identity - the immortal being known as Myself or more specifically as *an immortal Soul*. I like any other immortal Soul am an integral portion of God who has incarnated on Earth in order to serve IT in the land of everyday physicality.

Third, and the most significant and revered aspect of ourselves: as an immortal Soul, I, like all immortal Souls, am a component part of and thus a representative of Divinity here on Earth.

This, then, is My full and integrated biography, revealed in all three of My major aspects: My everyday or earthly humanity, My identity as an immortal Soul and My heritage as an integral component of The Lord. [1]

A Sacred Amalgam

As an immortal Soul, I am currently presenting MySelf in the everyday world as the citizen named William. I enjoy and am learning a great deal in being William, yet he is only My latest embodiment or incarnation. My true identity - like you and every other incarnate now living on Earth - is that of an immortal Soul, an aspect of the eternal God. My particular Soul name is Aeneas. [2]

Together - I, the immortal Soul Aeneas and William - are in essence one identity, My inner immortal energies being expressed outwardly through My moral and visible counterpart. We are one and the same. When My outer mortal expression as William eventually dies, I Aeneas will honor his service - and then, following a review and perhaps some additional training, quickly petition The Lord to enable my Soul to be expressed outwardly in one more relatively unique incarnate or embodiment.

What will be his or her name, characteristics and outer appearance? That will depend on The Lord and the earthly couple IT chooses to produce My next human incarnate. It will also help if My next incarnate is able to build on the progress made by its 20,000 predecessors. More on that later.

In sum, as the moral William is intended to serve as My immortal Soul's current expression in and to the outer world, so will I do My best to

---

1 Please note that the references to The Lord, The Divine, God or Prime Source are interchangeable and equivalent.

2 If you would like to know your name as a Soul, then ask for it in prayer or meditation. Be attentive to any name that may appear to you, and if true, may then repeat itself your dreams or reading or spontaneous insights as you go about your daily business.

serve The Lord and ITs [3] priorities. We Souls are - after all - the mediums that urge our earthly carriers to act in accordance with the loving ways and desires of The Lord; We bear the responsibility to guide each of our incarnates into adding to and deepening the presence of The Lord throughout the physical universe.

Aspects and Components

We immortal Souls thus choose to appear as everyday human-citizens of the Earth. We are the incarnate persons you see in the mirror every morning. Yet as incarnates we know we are merely em-bodi-ments of our immortal Souls, moral stand-ins or human surrogates for our deeper and ever-lasting identities as immortal Souls and thus integral components of The Divine.

As incarnates, we go about our daily lives - looking and acting like students, parents, workers, whoever. Initially, most are very much aware of their spiritual identity as babies and young children but that instinctual awareness tends to fade as we become involved in the everyday tasks of daily living. As the years pass, however, most of us gradually regain our early sense of spirituality and realize we are here for something more, namely to use our everyday presence as a springboard for expressing and fulfilling a larger and deeper mission.

Neither way, a fact is a fact: as Souls, we are empowered to bring our heavenly identities to bear as we live our lives on Earth. If so, we will have done our best to sow the seeds of love and compassion in any setting in which we are placed.

---

3 Note the changes in the use of pronouns. The simple form of 'it', for example, is fine for references to an everyday or earthly incarnate. However, some capitalization - as in 'It' - is necessary when referring to the status of an immortal Soul. The full capitalization of 'IT' is reserved for the divine. The same is true for such personal pronouns as we, We and WE.

As a composite of the everlasting and the everyday, we are empowered to imprint the designs of heaven unto our earthly pursuits, doing our best to emulate the loving environment of Heaven.

In sum, We each represent the three components of a sacred trio.

* There is the everyday and moral *Me,* the individual who lives in our home and works at our job or vocation.

* Then there is the *Soul* - the immortal being created by The Divine as an integral aspect of IT's eternal being. Each Soul - through the process of incarnation - has been granted the right and responsibility to form and become an earthy incarnate. Thus does God have a way to express Itself in the external world of everyday reality by utilizing the process of incarnation to enable the cells or Souls of ITs cosmic body to become embodied as incarnates in the physical realm.

Ultimately there is Prime Source ITSelf, initially transcendent and thus is beyond the range of human understanding and vision. Prime Source, however, also chose to reveal ITSelf and became immanent or present in the everyday activities of the material world. And, as we shall see, IT did so by incarnating as the Master Soul - ITs designated representative in the physical realm, the Being who gradually unfolded on Earth and became known in its bifurcated universe as the male and female aspects of Yeshua-Mary.[4]

*Prime Source then utilized the process of incarnation to enable the cells or Souls of ITs cosmic body to become embodied as incarnates in the physical realm.

Thus is the sacred trinity - body, soul and spirit - manifest in each of us and in every person we meet. True to our heritage, every one of we soulful human beings has a sacred role to play during our relatively short stays on

---

4 Everything in our earthly reality is perceived as bifurcated or divided into a pair of opposites: male-female, up-down, on-off, high-low, now-forever, tall-short, etc.

Earth: as the earthly embodiments of our respective Souls, we are each empowered to serve as representatives of The Lord, imbued with the mission to express divine love and compassion as thoroughly and often as we can.

That little 'ol me' we may have underestimated and taken for granted - is in reality - a greatly empowered being, a real *some-Body, an everyday representative of the cosmic One* - commissioned by its Maker to uplift that portion of 'the Earth' in which it is placed - trusting in the empowerments of its underlying Soul and in the process learning how to love everyone and everything it encounters.

Soul in the Middle

Let's switch pronouns and make this even more personal. The impersonal *Me* used in the earlier paragraphs really means *you, the up front and personal* individual reading this book. You are an essential link in fulfilling The Divine's intention to transform how our world, society, neighborhood and family operates. Your actions enable you to link the nudging of the heavenly way to your intentions and actions on Earth.

How so? Well, you - as noted - are an embodiment of your immortal Soul, and as an immortal Soul you are one of the billions of the cells that comprise the cosmic organism we know as God or The Divine. You are a component of God and when embodied on Earth you become a representative of God. It is like the seamless connection between a grandparent (the eternal God), a parent (you as an immortal Soul and integral component of God) and now the child-incarnate as their embodied delegate on Earth.

The progression is a natural one: you are a representative of God, who in working through ITs constituent cells or Souls, created you as one of ITs earthly advocates of love and compassion. Your identity as a soulful person began in Heaven and is destined to return there once you in your current incarnate form have completed your particular mission in the earthly arena.

Ever check the obituaries? The name of 'God' has never appeared for God's essence is eternal - although some philosophers like Nietzsche reasoned that the notion of God seemed no longer operative in society. Neither has anyone ever found the name of your Soul (in William's case, *Aeneas*) listed there, for like all Souls, It is immortal. Ah - but note the obituaries continuous tally of names from every ethnic and cultural background - like Harry, Sally, Louisa, Ruth, Abdul, Xiu, Mary and Irv - all incarnate names temporarily chosen by their resident Souls to serve a purpose for a finite number of years.

As the incarnate of an immortal Soul, you - like all soulful incarnates - provide the critical connection between the Divine and the material domains. You - in combination with all the billions of other incarnates that preceded and will inevitably follow you - are commissioned to use your soulful empowerments and infuse as much love and compassion as you can into the settings in which you are placed. You - a relatively frail yet soulful and thus empowered incarnate - have been selected by God to infuse more and more of heaven's attributes into your everyday activities.

The purpose of your life - as a literal *in-carn-ation* of your immortal Soul - is to slowly but surely transform the Earth into a replica of Heaven. And you do so using your soulful instincts to think, feel and act with love, joy, forgiveness and compassion.

And there you thought you were merely a beloved parent, attorney, ballplayer, financier, worker or other kind of wonderful person. You may indeed bear one or more of those esteemed labels. But you are obviously much, much more. You are indeed a grand person, a composite of integrated identities, on assignment as an immortal Soul, and in essence a blessed delegate of the all-loving and eternal Divine.

The Adhesive

A special note on the glue that makes your three-part identity adhere so perfectly. It is the process devised by the Lord called incarnation which empowers immortal Souls, as constituent aspects of God, to encase themselves into an everyday mortal being and become the person who is now reading this book.

Given such an esteemed background, that makes you both an immortal Soul and a moral delegate of the Divine. This sacred process of incarnation has enabled you, an immortal Soul, to first form and then be infused into your newborn incarnate, thereby using your earthly facade to serve a divine mission and achieve a cosmic purpose.

We cannot affirm your reality often enough:

1. Outwardly, you appear as a living and breathing human being, equipped with a mind, body and emotions, who obviously has been chosen to exist during this present time and live at your particular location on Earth.

2. Inwardly, however, you are an immortal Soul, an integral and constituent part of the universal Divine.

3. Thus you are in your everyday involvements a designated delegate of The Lord, the cosmic *One, meaning you are* here on Earth with the mandate to do everything you to transform your everyday, earthly involvements into happenings that progressively advance the heavenly agenda of love and compassion.

The everyday *You* - living in your house, apartment or tent - are nothing short of a tangible, human representative of Prime Source ITSelf. You were created through the process known as incarnation - the universal process by which You, through your immortal Soul, was empowered by God to arrange for the conception and birth of the being who now reads this paragraph - the one who responds to your name, lives at your address, thinks and acts as you do, bears the unique features of your face and has reason to celebrate your special alignment of mind, body and spirit.

A Learning Process

This means that anyone now reading this material is involved in a grand learning process, one that honors your spiritual heritage, identity and assignment. Your everyday human identity includes learning how to both intend and activate love and compassion in everything you do. Just in case it has not sunk in yet, here is your and everyone's living reality - written this time as a set of headlines:

You *are an integral part of Divinity, an immortal Soul whose creative unity of Body, Soul and Spirit is now empowered to achieve a series of spiritual objectives. Your everyday purpose is to fulfill the promises You made prior at the time of Your incarnation - which in essence amount to doing Your very best to help, support and love others despite the world's many temptations to do otherwise.*

Initially, you may have experienced yourself as just one more human being - talented, insightful, of course, but still just an average everyday human being. Sooner or later, however - often during your most difficult and introspective moments - you become increasingly aware of a deep inner and heightened spiritual impulse - leading you to realize you are indeed a creative delegate of The Lord God.

The growing awareness of your true identity and spiritual mission - focused on your particular set of capacities and talents - is what makes living your life such an adventure. Each moment and each situation present you with another opportunity to celebrate life by expressing your direct and soulful link with The Divine. In short, you are a person, a Soul and an integral aspect of God - a uniquely attuned composite who possesses great empowerments, a sacred mission and a divine identity.

Obviously, your three-part identity enables you to fulfill the mission clearly affirmed in the Bible: "Then God said: Let us make humankind in *our own image*, according *to our likeness*." (Genesis 1:26). This means you - like every one of your family members, friends and acquaintances - have been commissioned by The Divine to serve as ITs representative on Earth and thereupon express - and manifest - IT's creative and moral energy wherever you are placed and wherever you happen to roam thereafter.

Reality Check

We Souls have very good reason to be cheered by the constant arrival of the newborns that arrive on our planet everyday - fantastic new and highly equipped Souls, of course, yet perceived by most as merely the cherished children of some fortunate set of parents. Yet each one is really the incarnate of an immortal being, empowered to contribute to the evolution of our planet by building on what we, their predecessors, are still in the midst of achieving.

Of course, there is little in the historic record regarding the achievement of individuals and groups during the time when Earth's geographic plates were still tumbling into alignment eons ago when human life had not yet emerged. The only exception to that realization was summarized by Plato when he envisioned the moral choices later faced by the inhabitants of Atlantis (later also called Mu). Plato refers to the story told by Solon, the law-giver, who after traveling to Egypt and the city of Sais refers to an old priest who spoke of a power named Atlantis which fought against the powers (continental plates) of Europe and Asia some 9,000 years before. [5]

According to the Hebrew biblical record, the decisions rendered by God to create the universe suggest only that IT love - or was in some way be moved to form - the physical cosmos and 'breath life' into a 'living' being and 'his partner'. Nothing in the Bible clarifies God's motivation behind creation except that IT deemed it 'good'. [6]

A modern interpretation suggests Prime Source initiated the precursors of love and compassion when IT empowered Adam and Eve to leave the purely spiritual domain of the Garden and send them into the newly created earthly domain [7] - where they and their progeny could guide the animals and supervise the development of settlements and civilization. It appears that God further intended humanity to display love and

---

5 Plato, *Timaeus and Crito,* story told by Solon, summarized in *Wikipedia: Solon.*

6 Genesis 2: 7-18.

7 See William Francis Sturner. *Yeshua: The Continuing Presence of the Master Soul* (Osprey, FL: Other Dimensions, 2017).

compassion given ITs explicit creation of Adam and Eve and their capacity to generate the series of 'begots' and families that followed. [8]

The difficulties experienced by Adam and Eve's initial set of children demonstrated how problematic the process would be. Their son, Cain, murdered his brother Abel out of jealousy - although generations later, Enoch (their great, great grandson via their later son, Seth) epitomized love's finest values, walked with God and was assumed into Heaven. The subsequent list of biblical begets, however, seemingly struggled with humanity's enduring dilemma: how to quiet one's personal egotistical needs while choosing instead to live by the mysterious yet haunting desire to love and be loved by others.

Unfortunately, the human race has been faced with this dilemma throughout our recorded history - going back 5,000 years to the time of the Sumerians, Akkadians and Assyrians in Mesopotamia and the Egyptians in what has become the Middle East. Human beings, it seems, have always had to choose between shades of being selfish and invitations to be loving, between conceit and avarice on the one hand and kinship and forgiveness on the other. It is sliding scale, of course, but depending on the situation, we humans still tend to teeter between bloating our egos and passing judgement on others, and obeying our instinct to love and honor others no matter their race, creed, gender or social standing.

The continuing drama: will I, we, you - learn to affirm our true identity, spiritual heritage and spiritual mission, thereby deepening our commitment to act with empathy and good will? Or will we succumb to the temptation to inflate the ego, use intimidation versus loving others, and invent subtle and overt ways to undercut the expression of our spiritual potential?

---

8 See Genesis 5: 3-24.

Witness

The impact of such choices is clear when we current incarnates access the motivations of the untold number of Souls who have preceded us. One, seemingly there were folks who chose primarily to seek power and worldly riches. Others it appears, played it safe, choosing to lead a relatively comfortable life and taking few if any spiritual risks. And the third: there apparently were those who did follow their better angels and inclinations and caused a good deal of 'good trouble' [9] - even if it involved personal sacrifice.

It is in the third category that we find many or most of the world's spiritual leaders. Mention the names of any of the spiritual greats and their attributes quickly come to mind: Yeshua, who during His ongoing bodily incarnation has taken a series of actions that are contrary to the strict laws and codes Judaism - like His emphasis on forgiveness over condemnation and who He visited, prayed and dined with. Similarly, He has not followed the proclivity of the new Roman Catholic Church to mandate a theology based on generic sinfulness, clerical dominance and strict centralization of power. Yeshua - and Mary – instead have affirmed a revolutionary new credo based on love, forgiveness and compassion.

Then along came Buddha who gave up his royal title and the inheritances - to founded a form of mysticism that honored the inherent blessedness of every being (human and inanimate). Gandhi, on the other hand, was a devoted Hindu but his practice of self-sacrifice and compassion led to his being murdered by a young Hindu boy who accused Gandhi of political sedition and religious apostasy.

Another variation on the theme of committed spirituality is Francis of Assisi: a Roman Catholic monk who gave up a life of promised luxury, was visited directly by God on several occasions, became a mystic, lived in

---

9 The phase used by Representative John R. Lewis, Dem. Ga., civil rights icon and hero.

and professed poverty and became the patron of ecology and animals. Then there also is the itinerant Japanese mystic and monk, Basho; Dietrich Bonhoeffer, the protestant minister who faithfully upheld the principles of love in the face of Hitler's brutality; the American Helen Keller, technically blind and mute yet who inspired countless others as she learned to speak and communicate with ease and wisdom; and Mother Teresa, an avowed Christian who founded homes and clinics throughout India as part of her dedicated care for the impoverished.

Such incarnate souls are the sacred ones - yet they are only a few of the spiritual adepts who emerged in each generation and every culture. Who would you add to the list? Who has inspired you, served as your hero or heroine, is a living example of the kind of person you admire and whose traits you wish to develop and express? Could it be that some of your friends, family members and associates exhibit similar traits of acceptance, kindness, understanding and empathy - and honors everyone no matter how diverse his or her looks, language or societal standing.

Social Impacts

Look as well at the many social movements that have over time encouraged - and inspired - millions to galvanize action to uphold the principles of love and compassion. Despite the occasional shortcomings displayed by some leaders and movements, look at the contributions each have made to honoring what is surely considered spiritual behavior. Putting theological issues aside (frequently the source of bickering between various churches and creeds), many leaders and their religious organizations have chosen to respect both the diverse animate and inanimate expressions of Life.

Thus has the energy of goodness and love made its advance. For example, throughout ancient history, vengeance was the standard used to amend any wrong done to your family or tribe. The Jews greatly modified the usual standard of untrammeled brutality when they adopted the less grievous standard of 'an eye for an eye' (Exodus 21:23-27). Any response to a grievance would thus only approximate the harm received; not 'death for an eye' or slaughter for a minor grievance. That tempered 'standard' was also adopted by the Babylonian King Hammurabi (1810-1750 BCE) - as published in his Code of 1780 BCE, Paragraph 230. Later Roman Law also adopted a significant substitute for vengeance - and set the mark of compensation for an injury as 'an equivalency' (which could be administered bodily but which emphasized retribution in some material way or in a term of service). Christianity superseded that standard when Yeshua in the Sermon on the Mount (Matt. 5; 38-9) urged His followers to 'turn the other cheek'. Later, Islam also urged forgoing retribution entirely, doing so out of charity and in atonement for one's own sins. [10]

Obviously, these standards and those adopted by the many other religions and philosophies have not been followed universally throughout the many ages and cultures of society. But many of those who violated the modern norms of a sane and moral society have been found guilty and been punished severely, while many others - like Stalin, Hitler, Mussolini, Mao and Pol Pot (who perpetuated genocide on what he designated as the so-called 'unwanted portions' of the Cambodian society' from 1963-1991) were at least condemned by society.

The issue of what standard applied has seemingly varied in each situation. The atrocities committed by the Russians in Syria - and most recently - in the Ukraine - for example, have been condemned by the Assembly of the United Nations but - thus far (as of November 21, 2022) - have had little effect on the aggressive actions of Putin's Russia. Still we have reason to celebrate the ever expanding nature of society's compassionate intentions despite the occasional backsliding and contradictions. Today we at least affirm the progress society has made in adopting standards of justice, and decrying the deviations that were rarely even acknowledged in

---

10 For examples of what is known as 'retribution justice', see Wikipedia, 'Eye for an eye.'

earlier historic periods. So we carry on in the knowledge and conviction that we are not only moving in the right direction but doing so in concert with the continuous energy and now long acknowledged visions of the best among us.

The Two As One

Remember: each of us - and the many personalities we have been as previous incarnates – are merely the latest incarnates of our age-old immortal Souls. We are simply aligned in new clothing. In fact, we are all analogies of that twin relationship - such as William is the current incarnate or outer expression of My perennial immortal Soul, Aeneas. Yet you and your Soul are also one. And at the moment, we all live and work on Earth yet were originally - and still are - from Heaven.

As an immortal Soul now embodied in an earthly incarnate, I Aeneas and thus my incarnate William, are really complimentary aspects of The Divine, literal cells in the cosmic body of Prime Source yet also manifest as a human person living on Earth. As such, we are empowered as Divinity's ambassadors to the physical domain since our incarnate expressions carry our soulfulness into our human form. Thereby My divine Soul (or My Self) has not only produced and expressed Itself in the earthly arena as a corporal presence. It has also enabled the very local Me to be present in the everyday world of materiality.

Becoming an incarnate is not an easy assignment, however. Once we Souls obtain Prime Source's explicit 'go-ahead' or consent, we consent to the characteristics and placement of our desired embodiment and prepare it to be birthed into the wondrous yet potentially perilous area of the planetary universe. The spiritual mantra, 'As above, so below' is complemented with the phrase: 'As below, so Above'; 'in the physical domain as in the realm of Spirit'; and 'On 'Earth as it is in Heaven'.

The Drama of Everyday Life

Given his divine heritage, My incarnate William is predisposed to live a life of loving intentions and rightful actions. Yet as an incarnate he is also invested with free will – meaning that although he is the carrier of My immortal Soul, he is also capable of ignoring My advice and acting in ways contrary to his true and soulful identity.

Therein lays the source of the ensuing drama. The physical domain is filled with temptations to discard the goals and visions selected by our respective Souls prior to being birthed into physical reality. Thereafter choices abound: as human beings, we can ignore the training we received prior to being incarnated and thus brush off such soulful intentions in part or whole. Or as incarnate Souls We can strive to live an earthly life devoted to the god-like attributes of love and compassion - as originally intended.

In short, our soulful incarnates are perfectly free during their personal stays in the material realm to succumb to the pressures of earthly living: even going so far as to indulge in the so-called 'deadly sins' – pride, greed, wrath, envy, lust, gluttony and sloth - or any of their nuanced extensions: becoming vindictive, hurting or defaming others for personal gain, seeking vengeance, and even becoming so indignant or proud that we deny the Divine and our true soulful identity.

In the rush of events, we can become susceptible to any number of actions which can derail our loving missions, damage the essence of who we really are and undercut the reason for our placement here on Earth. We face multiple temptations – in big, little and disguised ways - every day. Despite the enticements and at times seductive nature of the incarnate life, however, most of We soulful human beings manage to embrace the invitations of our divine heritage, and actually learn how to display great spiritual affection and empathy for those we meet during our short but vivid stays on Earth.

Body, Soul, Divine

As human beings, we are constantly aware of our egos and our power to choose our intentions and select our behaviors. Once we act, we also face the feedback our attitudes and actions have on others. Our sense of ego - our personal, earthy identity - also monitors, measures and then evaluates how we feel about whatever and whomever we happen to experience. Inevitably we place a value on almost everything we encounter, judging each experience on an approximate scale of wonderful or love - to 'no-no-no' or bad and not to be repeated. Throughout the process, our egos register our thoughts in our brains, our feelings in our hearts and memories registered in those parts of our bodies that were immediately involved or affected.

It should come as no surprise then that the experiences shared in this book are those of the incarnate, William – the name given to him by his parents, the physical beings who in their physical union helped to activate the intentions of my Soul and give birth to the little 'ol' mortal me'.

The thoughts, intentions and actions subsequently experienced by the ego identified as *William on the mundane level, are then* simultaneously experienced by Me, Aeneas, the immortal Soul who formed and now guides the actions taken by His incarnate. As noted, We have become one and the same entity, two sides of the same coin.

My embodiment or incarnate, 'William' – was formed in order to receive My abiding Soul - also known to spiritual adepts as 'the Self' - the appellation used by Carl Jung, the famed Swiss psychologist. In spiritual terms 'the Self' is the 'Spirit' or 'Soul' that is embedded in the human psyche through the process of incarnation. It is synonymous with Jung's archetype of the center as well as the total circumference of a person's psyche, the reality that embraces both the conscious and the unconscious totality of our being. The totality is symbolized by the circle and the mandala. [11] It is

---

11 See C.G. Jung, *Two Essays on Analytical Psychology* (Collected Works 7, par. 274).

the best descriptor of My essence - and the role I, Aeneas, play in uniting My incarnate with Our God to form the *Sacred Trio*.

As it was with Me and My incarnate, so it has been for you and your abiding Soul, generation after generation, empowered Souls upon empowered Souls ceaselessly creating their next incarnate - all in service to The Lord and ITS desire to complete a spiritual transformation in and of our wondrous physical domain. [12]

The Soul

This brings us to the history of the formation of soulfulness. I, like you, was one of a billion particles or cells of The Lord when IT decided to expand ITs transcendent presence into the cosmic spheres to the immanent or everyday domain of the here and now. Thus, It devised the process of incarnation to enable such particles of ITSelf to form and then embody themselves into human beings in the physical realm. As noted, the being called *William* is now serving as My latest incarnate.

At this juncture, you may be asking yourself: what is my *true* name, not the one given me by my biological parents but the name of my formative and immortal Soul, the one that creates and underlies every one of your Soul's incarnations? It is one way that you, your Soul's latest incarnate, may open direct communication with your abiding Soul.

Being named - in this case, having been named by the Lord is itself an awesome process. So 'tis time you updated Yourself and formally acknowledged the name given to You as an immortal Soul. The process of retrieving that name, of course, begins with Your asking for It. Although the name may not dawn on you immediately - It surely will appear - perhaps

---

12 In March, 2016 a song composed and sung by G-Eazy and Rebs Rexha entitled 'Me, My Self and I' reached the Billboard Hot 100 song hits. The title certainly evoked some of the spiritual themes outlined here although the lyrics were confined mostly to the personal aspect.

as a gift when you least expect it, during a particular dream or in a name that just keeps popping up as you go about your everyday business.

Divine Cells and Mortal Beings

Bear in mind: our respective Souls are immortal although not eternal - for They too were once created by The Divine. And they are not divine unto Themselves but share in the Lord's divine nature - being merely cells or particles in ITS cosmic presence. And as You surely know, immortal Souls love to respond to The Lord's call to infuse themselves in their mortal incarnates and thus 'people' the universe with our everyday stand-ins.

Obviously, Our incarnates are merely mortal beings who are intended to play a significant role but who are not intended to live forever. They are, however, meant to play a role in the culture and historic time in which they are placed and thus do what they can to add to the enhancement and sanctification of the created realm. Being mortal, the likes of William and any person reading this manuscript will eventually surrender its mortal capacities, at which time its sponsoring Soul will return to Heaven, receive an evaluation of Its most recent embodiment, and thereafter await The Lord's encouragement to be infused into one more incarnate. [13]

It is no wonder then that Our soulful incarnates appear in all shapes and sizes - given the circumstances of the changing times, the lessons our sponsoring Souls still need to learn, and the evolving needs and purposes of The Lord. As you will see in the following sections of this book, my Soul - like yours - has appeared as a range of varied incarnates throughout the centuries.

Like any Soul, Aeneas remembers the names and major experiences of all of Its earlier embodiments; He carries that historic memory with Him,

---

13 For a review of the learning processes involved, accompanied by both whimsical and realistic case studies, see the author's book entitled, *Kindred Spirits* (East Aurora, NY: Other Dimensions, 2011).

installing the record of all of His earlier embodiments in the base of the skull of each successive incarnate. As we will see, the stored memories contribute to the makeup, skills, interests and proclivities of each successive embodiment. Thus, do most of William's and My experiences fit into the patterns established earlier during our respective histories.

As we will see, both William and I have a tendency (1) to question authority, (2) jettison one's early devotion to a religion in order to explore a variety of spiritual alternatives, (3) trust in our capacity to receive and convey healing energy, and (4) focus Our presentational skills on Our spiritual insights and experiences. More on each of these themes in subsequent chapters as we deal more explicitly with William's tenure as an incarnate (Me) and My cumulative record as an immortal Soul (My Self).

Prime Source

So much for our introductory remarks regarding the first two parts of our Sacred Trio, namely William and his immortal Soul, Aeneas. Now 'tis time to also introduce and honor the third aspect, namely the foundational aspect of the entire universe, the creator of the cosmos, the process of incarnation and the physical world - namely God, aka The Divine, The Lord or Prime Source. This ubiquitous, eternal and divine Creator is the ever-present and energizing presence of the universe. It is the only entity entitled to affirm ITs eternal presence as *I AM*. It is also epitomized in our sacred trinity simply as *I*.

The eternal being - or *I* - empowered ITs component Souls to carry ITs spiritual essence of love into the material realm. As noted, William's immortal Soul - Aeneas – along with the billions of other Souls, including yours - are components or cells in the cosmic reality of the Divine. We have been are empowered, assigned and pre-wired to create embodiments of Ourselves and thus do whatever We can in the physical realm to make it more and more like Our true homes in heaven.

And so has HE/SHE/IT - the cosmic, transcendent and other-worldly Divine - made ITSelf manifest or immanent in this everyday world. IT has done so through the creation and subsequent infusion or incarnation into the physical world of the twin Master Souls, Jesus or Yeshua and Miriam or Mother Mary. [14] After serving throughout Earth's history in multiple iterations, both Yeshua and Mary fulfilled THEIR destiny during the biblical period and became the dual or masculine and feminine aspects of the Master Soul. [15]

As the worldly, grounded or immanent extensions of the transcendent Divine, they now serve in perpetuity here among us on Earth (as well as the rest of the created universe). Given their divine status as the surrogates of Prime Source, Yeshua and Mary bring the transcendent Spirit of The Lord into manifestation in the here, and the now, and the everyday.

We will continue to point to The Divine as the prime or supreme *I* in our sacred equation. Given Their heritage, however, we may also refer to Yeshua and Mother Mary as Divine *and* present in earthy circumstances - both transcendent and immanent, sacred in the heavenly realm as well as ever-present in everyday materiality.

All three aspects of our sacred and interactive Trio have thus been identified and introduced. We will now explore the workings of each - relying first, on the words and experiences of the current incarnate, the mortal

---

14 Jesus is here referred to as *Yeshua*, the Anglicized version of the equivalent Hebrew name Jeshua The name of Mary, of course, is the Anglicized version of the Hebrew equivalent of Miryam or Miriam, which may have originated from the Egyptian language; it is likely the derivative of the root *mr* "love or beloved".

15 The Master Soul is present in perpetuity throughout the universe. On Earth, IT is present in the twin (male and female) form of Yeshua and Mary in keeping with the binary or bifurcated nature of life on Earth (big-small, hot-cold, etc). Throughout the rest of the universe, however, the Master Soul is manifest under a name or names that are in keeping with the nature of the particular planetary, solar or cosmic system in which It is being expressed.

element known as 'Me' or William; then on the previous appearances or embodiments of the immortal Soul, the formative element, 'My Self' or Aeneas; and finally on the causative element, focusing on the workings and wisdom of Divinity - as manifest in Yeshua and Mary, the twin aspects of the Master Soul.

Telling the Story

This then is a love story in which a mere incarnate by the name of William recognizes and celebrates the Soul energy that forms and continues to guide him; the divine particle or Soul which honors ITs creator by fulfilling ITs promise to incarnate; and God ITSelf as IT continues to deepen and expand ITs presence throughout the cosmos. The ceaseless manifestation of the Sacred Trio - our seamless composite of 'Body, Soul and Divinity - also known as 'Me, My Soul and My Lord' - constitutes the bone, blood and sinew of Life as manifest throughout the universe.

Each aspect of the trinity contributes to the cohesive sense of the Whole. Each facet is integral to the psycho-spiritual identity known throughout the cosmos as the realm of the sacred. The everyday incarnate referred to as *Me,* is the embodiment of the immoral Soul that formed it, which in turn is an integral aspect of the seamless and ubiquitous Divine.

Chapter One. The Mortal Element:

The Everyday Embodiment Known as '*Me*'

William It Is

AND SO WE INVESTIGATE THE DEVELOPMENT OF THE PERSON-
ALITY CALLED WILLIAM, THE NAME OF MY CURRENT EMBOD-
IMENT. BEAR IN MIND, I THE IMMORTAL SOUL NAMED AENEAS, AND
My incarnate, are one and the same being. It is just that I, Aeneas, a cell or
particle in the cosmic divinity, is from heaven and has since time immemorial resided there. The Lord created the process of incarnation, however, to
enable Us to embody a portion of Our soulfulness into the humans born
in the physical realm and become as one with the new incarnates.

This, of course, is where William comes in. He is an incarnate now
serving as My expression or personality in this material realm. We will
outline the events of William's life as well as his dominant skills, drawbacks
and concerns, and then turn our attention to the list of his predecessors,
each one of which was designed to meet My developmental needs at particular points in My history.

You - being your immortal Soul's current incarnate or personality
are invited to follow along - as you recall and ponder the aspects of your
three-part identity: (1) your earthly personality; (2) your actions as an

immortal Soul, and (3) how you are honoring Your identity as a representative of The Lord.

So let's start with your current personality of sense of Me, in this case - *William*. For the sake of clarity, it seems best to describe events in William's life in the third person. As best as I can recall, the themes of religion and spirituality entered into William's consciousness while he was still a child. He was a good kid, did very well in school, yet upon completing his homework joined his teammates in the streets of the north-central area of the Bronx to use every corner, stoop, curb, car fender, sign and crevice they could find to invent one game after another. Of course, that included stick ball and then 'half-ball' once the pinkish ball finally broke in half.

It was not until high school, however, that William became a dedicated member of the Catholic Church, going to Mass every day - and becoming the family's sole representative at Sunday services. Meanwhile his father faithfully said the Rosary, his mother attended a series of novenas, and his older brother played baseball constantly and became a local hero.

Limits of Allegiance

William's enthusiasm for the Church remained constant throughout college, then as a graduate student at the University of Wisconsin, and subsequently as an intern at The Washington Post.

It was not until he later returned to graduate school - at Fordham University, a Catholic University so less - that doubts first appeared - and then blossomed. One crack in the automatic regimen led to a series of others, until he gradually pulled away from Catholicism in both practice and sentiment. Finally, he left the Church after being condemned by a Catholic group for opposing the bishop's call for aid to religious schools - which William, as a student of constitutional law, vigorously opposed. Thereafter, there was no turning back.

He then experimented with a series of alternatives, reading books on Buddhism, Taoism and Hinduism, keeping a diary that recorded his daily selection of *I Ching* symbols, going for readings in Tarot and numerology and finally embracing a practice of meditation and prayer. He yearned for and gradually entered into a direct conversation with The Lord: no clerics, no theology, no mandatory rituals, cultivating his desire to learn how to love unconditionally, forgive immediately and trust in each life's changing fortunes.

The transition from a structured hierarchical system to an untethered romp through the diversities of spirituality was gradual but once was made left William feeling free to align with the open-ended flow of the divine. He spent less and then no time kneeling with folded hands, instead finding delight in the free exploration of a universe he previously had not even noticed. [16]

There was even a point in which he felt he had crossed over into the what he experienced as the realm of 'self-affirmation' - viewing himself inherently as a spiritual being versus the old religious habit of confessing to a list of alleged shortcomings to some invisible clerical intermediary. It was then that he became an advocate for his new way of life. He did not wish to be a *provocateur* - overly pushing or pulling someone into his way of thinking. Rather he saw himself as an *evocateur,* inviting others to join him in affirming their newfound discoveries and spiritual experiences. Rather than relying on a Missal or a catechism, he re-invested in the wondrous joys of nature, the profound insights of friends (versus the bookish sermons of priests), and heeding the lessons learned through everyday experience.

Second Giant Leap

In early June, 1982, William made what turned out to be another enormous leap in faith. It happened as he was preparing to offer a workshop

---

16 For a more specific rendering of William's experiential road to 'spirituality versus religiosity', see William F. Sturner, *Trust Your Immoral Soul: A Guide to Spiritual Living* (Amherst, NY: Other Dimensions and CreateSpace, 2012 and 2016).

for a conference of the Creative Problem-Solving Conference (CPSI) in Buffalo NY. The annual gathering attracted several hundred people for a week of workshops designed to help the participants explore and enliven their personal and professional lives. This year William 'took a chance' and volunteered to offer a workshop on 'The Spiritual Journey' – a sign that he was indeed ready to express his growing participation in spiritual beliefs and practices.

He sensed what he wanted to do - but had no idea on how to do it - that is until a week before: 'Use music and imagery to encourage everyone's intuitive sense of the spiritual process'. Why not? He had for years offered workshops that encouraged folks to use colored pens, drawings and clay to explore their personal and professional lives as they responded to various kinds of music. 'Why not do the same for this new focus on spirituality!' So, he selected 11 excerpts from his collection of vintage 78" and 45" recordings (the state of the art in 1982), and the outline of the workshop was complete. By-the-way: he still has the forty-fine minute tape (the revolutionary medium of the day) that he originally used to record those selections.

And it worked: some twenty-five persons signed on, using pens and crayons to record their own experience with the themes of religion and spirituality. To facilitate their responses, William played a variety of mood of music: pensive, dreamy, spritely, fantastic, even slow and dreary pieces to help folks recall and deal with any periods of blockage and resistance.

The workshop proved to be so popular that over the next 20 years the initial two-hour session expanded to four hours, and participation grew from the initial 25 participants to overflow sessions of over 400 attendees. By the fifth year William was also using five-foot Bose speakers to broadcast the music used to support the incorporation of lots of movement, dance and body sculpting. [17] In short, he was able to go public regarding his exploration of all things spiritual. He had passed the Rubicon.

Impacts

That workshop thereby encouraged William to continue trusting his intuition, and it became his model for dealing with a host of related issues: the relationships he cultivated, the books he read and then wrote, the time he devoted to prayer and meditation, the images he cultivated and the openness he continued to display toward a series of new ideas and activities. One door after another opened as he waved 'goodbye' to that which no longer 'spoke' to him - namely the Church or any structured religion that believed in sin and inherent degradation of the human soul; their adoption of orate rituals, complex theological doctrines and strict hierarchical systems only made things worse.

Thereafter, he increasingly - then fully - dropped his earlier allegiance to the the Catholic Church, enabling him to explore The Divine wherever IT appeared - which turned out to be in aspects of Hinduism, Buddhism, mysticism, tarot and astrology. The emerging synthesis placed priority on that which honored the paramount importance on love and compassion - and minimized if not eliminated allegiance to pronouncements and structures, clerically dominated rituals and ceremonies, layers of 'should's' and 'should nots' and any notion that the biblical story of Adam and Eve portrayed the corruption of the very soul of humankind.

---

17 For music, he initially relied on the likes of Neal Diamond, Brian Eno and Beethoven. As the length of the workshop grew, he gave increasing emphasis to excerpts from Stravinsky's 'Rite of Spring', Shostakovich's 'Gadfly', the songs of Suzi Quatro and the Mormon Tabernacle Chorus, Offenbach's 'The Tales of Hoffman' and the music from such movies as 'Witness' and 'The Mission'. He even flowed with the technology over the years, downloading music from his cds directly onto his computer.

Simple, clean, direct, yet open to God's continuing guidance: that was the prism through which William refocused his life. Above all, he realized that he had a right to refuse parroting the beliefs of others - no matter how revered. Instead, he affirmed himself to be an open and interactive 'tribe of one' - ever receptive to new learnings as he sought out and communed with kindred spirits steeped in the energies of love and compassion.

En route, William grappled with one clue or footprint after another. His mantras became: *'Trust yourself for you are a child of The Lord'*, and *'Affirm* the *Spirit that permeates every aspect of life'*. So did 'Follow Your Bliss' - the bottom line of Joseph Campbell's inspired writings - influence both the books William read and subsequently authored. No one insight or person provided the 'answer' but the gist of many of them supported William growing realization that his - and everyone's - spiritual journey was governed by the urge to simplicity. No longer was anything assumed or preordained. Instead - everything, everything, *everything* offered an inkling, a hint, a potential clue to the glories of Spirit as revealed in the everyday process of living.

Natural Revelations

Gradually these natural revelations of life were experienced as direct nudging and invites of The Lord. Nature, divinity and William were beginning to feel like they were joined at the hip. Cumulatively his glimpses into the mystic realities of his Soul prompted him to realize who he really was: an everyday being who - finally - had the good sense to acknowledge and affirm his Soul's pre-eminent identity and capacity to guide Its latest incarnate into deeper connections with the varied aspects of the Divine.

Thus did William begin to realize consider the he, like all other soulful incarnates, was really a facet of Spirit. And given the universal presence of Spirit, we were capable of encountering some manifestation of God everywhere we went, within everyone we met and in everything we see and experience. Spiritual identity, moreover, was a function of being alive: every human possessed the soulful bona fides that enabled them to tune into and accept the multi-faceted presence of Spirit. One's sense of involvement in the ongoing display of The Lord was affirmed whenever one looked around to notice and affirm ITs continuous unfolding.

It came as no surprise then that William came to consider a walk among a stand of trees, playing with a child, romping with a dog, or chatting spontaneously with a neighbor to approximate a 'religious' experience - since the presence of God was no longer confined to some designated building. Everything, everything - everything testified to the love of God, was equally special, part of Spirit's endless vitality. Distinctions in time could even evaporate during bouts of living in the Now. Whether entranced by memories of the past or by visions of the future, he also had the withal to see Spirit as the seamless feature of whatever was *here and now* and fully in the moment.

Trusting in his intuitive insights, his love of experiential learning and his natural tendency to covet his alone time, William gradually developed confidence in his sense of spiritual identity. Whatever his natural capacities, they were now focused on attending to his sense of soulfulness and following its counsel.

Soulfulness

The tumblers were now being more closely aligned - giving William greater access to his intuition and the whisperings of his Soul. The mere incarnate finally realized he really *was* a Soul who was displayed in the everyday as a specific embodied form. The realization initially staggered him. Although his true identity was implied by each of his recent experiences - he had not yet internalized it or formally affirmed it. Finally, he was on the brink of reaching a new - and dare we say - greatly deepened and extended sense of identity.

Of course, he did not realize at the time that even his more intensive sense of identity still fell far short of the full reality, something he did not fully internalize until he had the opportunity to uncover the insights outlined in the next two chapters, namely those dealing with *My Self or Soul and the Big I or God.* Only then was he finally able to affirm that he was not only an immortal Soul, but *actually an incarnate or carrier of an immortal Soul - a celestial being dressed temporarily as a human being - an integral part of the same* God revealed earlier to Moses as the eternal *I AM*.[18]

The audacious title of this book affirms his - and your - sacred identity. We are each designated deputies of The Lord - our worldly extensions mere fleshy inflections of the formative aspects of The Big **I.** As extensions of Our immortal Souls, these temporary embodiments of Ours are also facets of the eternal and transcendent Prime Source. That means each of we humans now living on Earth are particles of God, manifestations of IT in the material world. That also makes us part and parcel of Yeshua and Mary, the twin aspects of the Master Soul - who are none other than an earthly version of the heavenly Lord God ITSelf.

In short, *you and I* are personal representatives of The Lord - here to work with the billions of other incarnates, contributing what we can - for as long as our mortal lives last - to the continuous evolution of the cosmos. Like William, we temporary incarnates are capable of becoming aware of the depths of our supporting cast: created by our immortal Souls, we are here temporarily on a planet that needs our love and devotion. The resistance will be great, the temptations will be around every bend, and the time allotted to us very short. Yet our mission is of the greatest importance, our empowerments many, our respective Souls are guiding us and Yeshua and Mary are ever at our side.

The Unfolding

I, William the incarnate, am now 86 years old. As a youngster growing up in the Bronx - and then progressively a journalist and workshop

---

18 The Lord told Moses that IT's name was "I Am that I Am". Exodus 3:14

leader - I may have been 'religious' but was not aware that my Soul was immortal and thus an aspect of The Divine. As noted, my awakening to reality was slow one and unfolded in stages - as if the universe did want to overwhelm me with the truth too quickly. I - perhaps like you - was slowly paced into that fuller realization, finally letting go of the assumption that my ego was my sole identity.

I progressed - I now realized - by following the hints and clues I received at each point of my unfolding. For example, I worked to recall the facets of my personal unconscious, keeping track of my major experiences as well as my day and night dreams. Gradually I also became interested in what Carl Jung called 'the collective unconscious' - which reportedly consisted of the depth and expansiveness of our common or universal psyche - including our encounters with the other-worldly.

I also monitored my spontaneous writings and drawings - the words and images 'automatically' gifted to me without their being consciously invoked. Slowly, I learned to honor my intuition, trust its capacity to unearth moments of great clarity and even invited me to explore ideas and the lives of people I had never heard of before.

Cumulatively, I found myself 'suddenly' saying 'yes' to what I theretofore had assumed was 'silly and 'impossible' - namely automatic writing, namely trusting in whatever came to mind and typing it out on my computer. Lo and behold, I simply allowed my fingers to register whatever came to mind, typing out whole paragraphs and then pages of insights and information never available to me before.

I can only describe it as my ego opening up to the pulsations of my Soul, thus enabling me to access sources I previously was not aware of. Apparently, I no longer had to rely on materials I had gathered previously or on any notes or outlines I had prepared earlier. Unexplainably, whatever mental and emotional intermediaries I normally used to prompt my writing had - at least momentarily - been rendered superfluous.

Suddenly I started to understand the meaning and significance of what earlier were merely theoretical terms: spirituality, transformational, *ego, Soul, The Lord* and *the personal and collective* unconscious. Alas, greater degrees of faith – alias *trust* - urged me to venture ever deeper, accessing realms of spirituality through meditation and contemplation, thereby producing ever more wondrous insights - like those that have sparked the writing of this book.

Then I even began to recall My (or My Soul's) incarnation as John of Jerusalem - whose travels with Yeshua and then Mother Mary were recorded in two books that resulted from hours and days of automatic writing.[19] It should come as no surprise then, that the theses and affirmations set forth in this book are also rendered by Aeneas, as narrated this time by William, Its latest incarnate or manifestation. [20]

The cumulative impact increasingly prompted William to recognize what was fast becoming his main calling: to make sense of his life experiences, to share what he uncovered and learned, and thereby to invite others to follow a similar process and reveal the incarnate experiences of their respective Souls. 'Learning how to love, learning how to contribute and learning how to discover and express one's Soul identity are indeed the essential tasks of our short-lived tenure on Earth. If lived with verve and commitment, our Souls will then wend their way back to Heaven once our earthly embodiments have completed their significant yet temporary missions.

---

19 *Yeshua: The Continuing Presence of the Master Soul;* and The *Return: Traveling With Mother Mary, op.cit.*

20 It certainly seems that the connection between William and Aeneas, described earlier as two sides of the same coin, totally meld together or are revealed in total unity during such 'automatic writing' - enabling a direct communication between our heavenly and earthly energies or what Carl Jung would call our collective or universal consciousness and our incarnate or everyday consciousness.

Everyday Reality

In becoming aware of his true identity as the carrier of an immortal Soul, William became ever more aware of his everyday empowerments as an incarnate. Oh my: it was a wonder unto itself to realize that we each have the capacity to convert what we used to consider just another event into the realization of its miraculous nature.

The cycles of such conversions depend on the attitude with which we engage such ordinary tasks - noting the everyday task and then parenthetically its symbolic or spiritual meaning: washing one's clothing (being ready to enter into the world), vacuuming the house ('cleansing the temple'), shopping for food (upholding the cohesion between body, mind and Soul), coordinating a set of family activities (celebrating our fellow incarnate-Souls), completing otherwise mundane tasks (sustaining a healthy environment), learning about people and events around the world (updating the foci of our love and compassion); and all the everyday happenings like stopping to greet our neighbors, stooping to swell the roses, and choosing to appreciate the stream of e-mails that wish you well (opportunities for our inner and outer Selves to be at one with the universe).

Without such a perspective, the issues of daily living can seem demanding and even annoying - silly distractions that divert us from the really important goals of making more money, bolstering our reputation and embellishing the mundane fortunes of life.

Sooner or later, we all seem to realize that the circumstances of our lives are part of a feedback system, reminding us to attend to the awesome nature of the immediate yet do so with a keen awareness of our heavenly identity and Its empowerments. We are capable of not only stumbling into the world each day or literally engaging and embracing it as a loving and playful companion. Each day our earthly domain offers us another chance to express the instincts of our Souls - choosing to focus on the spiritual dimension of every situation we encounter and thus help to create and experience.

The array mental, emotional and physical skills, abilities and automatic systems possessed by the personal Me have a place in the great scheme of things: to protect and enhance our circumstances in the everyday world, of course. But, as we shall see in the coming chapters, our empowerments have also been gifted to us as means to express our capacity to love and forgive, sing and dance, smile and celebrate - and in so doing help our Souls express their heavenly heritage and achieve their true destiny.

When viewed from the full context of Life, my sense of the incarnate Me would in great part be wasted if my powers were confined to merely the ephemeral interests of the day. Ultimately, my incarnation on earth is intended to serve the needs, desires and intentions of my immortal Soul - and thus our eternal God.

Serving the interests of the personal, earthly Me is really a test run for serving the interests of my Self, which in turn is a test run for how well My Soul is able to achieve the mission designed for It by Its divine overseer. So the question is: Can my sense of Me learn to operate so effectively that it enables my personal empowerments to serve the goals of my innate Soul? And will that embodied Soul in turn fulfill Its promise to support The Lord as IT expresses ITSelf in and through little 'ol incarnate Me and my 'everyday' life?

As we shall see, our physical, mental and emotional being - namely our sense of our personal Me - was not only formed to be our Soul's latest expression. You and I as incarnations were literally created to help the Soul - and thus The Lord - attain Its goals. The personal Me only realizes ITs full potential as it serves its spiritual identity and learns how use its sacred capacities to convert the everyday into the everlasting.

We soulful incarnates are ultimately slated to attend to and abide by the promptings of the Soul - evident in the spiritual standards of our conscience. All the attributes generally attributed to the personal Me are really devised to support the missions of My Soul. You and I were conceived and birthed in order to enable our Souls to create manifestations of love and thanksgiving in this physical realm. My personal attributes were conferred on Me by My Soul, as yours were on you - in order to help each and all of us express and expand the presence of The Lord here in the world of the everyday now.

Personal Focal Points

In my particular case, my Soul chose to form and then guide Me, William, to achieve the promises I made prior to my final birthing. Thus did It infuse a portion of Its soulfulness into my earthly incarnation - at which time we became one and the same.

As I proceeded from being a child to an adult, to a senior citizen (gulp!) - I chose to participate in a series of activities that focused on the issue of communication. It started with my writing for my elementary and then my high school and then college newspaper. By the time I was in college I had become an editor of the weekly newspaper, which led to my writing for industry as I completed a master's degree in communications, then becoming an assistant to the editor of a major metropolitan newspaper, and eventually the author of several books on creativity, transformation and spirituality. [21]

Going Deeper

When it came time for me to record my growing interest in and experience with the various themes of spirituality, I had already laid the groundwork for naturally sharing my thoughts in writing. So I not only focused more and more time on issues of the Spirit - reading and researching as I always did on anything that interested me. But now a new factor had slowly entered the scene - one that galvanized my attention and allowed me to write with greater ease and abandon than ever before.

---

21 See the biographical statement included in *Trust Your Immortal Soul*, noting the evolution of my interest in communication as well as religion and spirituality.

I speak now of my indebtedness to my Soul for prompting me to trust in and record many of the insights I received - prompted by my Soul and the spirits it could more easily access. As noted, it has been expressed most recently through automatic or inspired writing. For many years now, all I, William (or I, Aeneas - take your choice) need to do is sit in front of the computer - invoke the presence of Spirit, and within seconds, the thoughts, images, words and sentences come to mind - stopping only to catch egregious errors in spelling.

This so-called 'automatic' way of writing stunned me or William at first; lacking a vocabulary for such encounters, they now simply refer to the source of his latest books as 'otherworldly'. The process is not only energizing - for the words do flow revealing information and insights that William had not discovered in his readings or any other known source. Needless to say, the whole thing was and continues to be deeply humbling and profoundly moving.

A Step Back

Let's now take a step back and examine what it meant initially to view oneself as simply a free-standing ego who used the word and concept of 'religion' to make contact with what seems like an otherworldly entity that you and I and the world would normally refer to as 'God'.

Me is the usual pronoun, *my* and *mine* are the words my psychological sense of ego uses to describe *my* choices and possessions. The ego-identity refers to my embodiment in the physical sphere, the one who exhibits a certain pattern of mental and emotional capacities which it uses to select it's every day and long-range intentions, choices and activities - which in William's case has included the particulars of creating a career, getting married, helping to generate of two children and pursuing a career in communications and also living a varied and active schedule involving a great deal of travel.

What is most important about William's - and anyone's development - is that each aspect of it is the result of series of decisions made according to a fairly standard process: 'after acknowledging a particular need or desire, we would mentally explore our options and then choose a means to attain a particular goal.' The sequence of *aware-create-choice-action is* something we do millions of times a day as we develop our values, relationships, careers and sense of identity.

The Granular Level

Let's take that process to the granular level to better understand how impulses trigger a review of our options and finally the selection of a course of action. I have always been enthralled by the process, for example, of feeling thirsty and then wishing to get a drink of water, and then immediately reaching for a glass, turning on the facet, filling the glass with water and actually quenching my thirst. We invoke such a process automatically a thousand times a day as we honor a wish and then choose a course of action designed to satisfy the need.

A neurological explanation of how any thought translates into a set of actions is an elusive and mystifying one - yet we can describe the general sequence. A felt need sets off a series of impulses that activate within us an awareness of our reactions, possible choices and probable responses. In this case, the impulses are translated by the brain into electrical charges that automatically wind themselves through a set of neurological networks, invoking the muscles of one's arm, which activates the intention to find a glass, fill it with water and extend the glass to one's lips – all of which is followed by another process we call 'swallowing', causing the digestive system to do its thing: consuming the water and releasing a signal to the brain that our thirst has been quenched.

And that is only half of it. The same neurological and bodily responses are invoked each time we form an intention and proactively choose to pursue a desired action to achieve any result. These choices invoke the same set of instantaneous mind-body connections noted above - whether they apply to quenching one's thirst or the many actions needed to pursue a particular a job - no less executing as series of such decisions in pursuit of a career. Then there are all the specific decisions involved in traveling to see grandma, preparing a meal, becoming a devoted Episcopalian, moving to Maine or just across town, and so and so on.

Each mini and maxi experience is then stored in our memory (involving another set of electrical interactions), before being evaluated by us on any number of scales: efficiency, effectiveness, immediate or long-range gratification, whatever. Such evaluations then become the backdrop for acknowledging and focusing on whatever next gets our attention.

Gulp - And Holy Mackerel

It never dawned on me during my early years that such a set of internal systems even existed no less being essential to the process of living our lives. The intricate workings and seamless coordination between such a set of complex, automatic and seemingly miraculous systems was simply taken for granted. All I knew - and seemingly all I wanted to know at the time - was that 'something' was going on that enabled me to live and thrive, moment after moment, year after year. Beyond that, who cared - as long as I thought my needs were taken care of - that is until a series of missteps, annoyances and disappointments forced me to examine what was going on

The fact is: all day long, every day, everywhere, billions of people - adult and child, black-white-tan-red-and-yellow – all living in diverse cultures throughout the varied geographic areas of the world - go through the same impulse-to-action responses billions upon billions of times a day - oblivious to the easy unfolding of their mental and bodily systems - that is until 'something' went repeatedly or radically wrong. It is only then that we became introspective, slowed down, took inventory and began to examine the values, motives and assumptions that govern our choices.

Taking Stock

If you ever doubt that you are using your heritage and all the empowerments that come with it, spend a moment reflecting on your capacity to do the following: think of lifting your arm and gently pat your face. Now, how indeed did you do that? What gives you the power to instantly follow your wish with actions that fulfill your intention?

And think of how often you exercise everything from simple activities to a series of them taken in rapid sequence – like getting into your car, listening to some music, chatting with a friend, making turns to the right and then the left, stopping at a restaurant, adjusting your clothing, swallowing one forkful of food after another, reaching to scratch an itch, paying the check before driving back home, feeling some indigestion, swallowing an antacid as you play with your children and pet the dog, then laughing out loud while watching tv, hearing the ting of your i-phone and then sending a return e-mail, discarding your slippers after finding them too warm, feeling the coolness of your sheets, waking at night to use the bathroom and on and on and on, every day in every way, making millions of decisions involving the intricacies of choosing and taking a series of actions, a gazillion times a week, billions of times over a lifespan, all initiated and completed through an untold number of easily coordinated decisions that you innocently and blithely assume will always unfold as intended. Zow!

Perhaps we might now refer to such automatic workings of the mind-body connections with such words as *stupendous* and *unbelievable* – especially given the reality that we usually take each manifestation of the process *for-granted* – and do so minute after minute, hour after hour, day after day, year after year.

Modern science surely gives us explanations of these processes and how they create the information needed to fix any difficulties we have in closing the gap between wanting something and achieving it. Again: these processes take place every micro-second of every day - all over the world. Yet even our awakened awareness of the system's existence cannot answer the ultimate questions of exactly *how* it operates and *why*.

Enters the Soul

How indeed are these connections, transitions and transformations even possible? The scope of our bedazzlement increases exponentially when we view the seamless unity between our impulses and our human embodiments - in the context of our immortal Souls and the causative and creative genius of pure Spirit. There is no escaping such issues as we anticipate the full working of the Sacred Trio. And remember we are still dealing with only the first portion of that three-part sequence.

So we have already entered the realm of the super-incredulous, the land of the spiritual miracle in which the thoughts and actions of every living being are on display within each of us - every minute of every day.

Yet thank goodness for the immortal Soul embedded within us that helps us understand how Our psycho-material-spiritual entities operate. Once formed bodily in accordance with the general specs outlined by our immortal Soul and approved by The Lord, the future incarnate awaits the infusion of its Soul at the time the fetus emerges from the womb. Let's go through this again - step by step. Once formed bodily in accordance with the general specs outlined by our immortal Soul and approved by The Lord, the future incarnate awaits the infusion of its Soul at the time the fetus emerges from the womb. Awareness of that fusion lasts through the first three years of the new child's life. Thereafter, the child's consciousness of Its abiding Soul fades as the everyday ego establishes its footing and assumes the lead in dealing with all the worldly situations it faces.

The fulcrum thus sways to the primary care and feeding of the body and mind - as the young organism negotiates its way through the myriad events involved in adjusting to family life, the trials and tribulations of making friends, the various levels of schooling, relating to the complications of sex, and in general learning how to balance one's individual needs and wishes with those of parents, friends and the many levels of society.

At each stage, the Soul's norms of love and compassion beckon to us but the impulse to develop a clear sense of Me also triggers a sense of selfishness and an appetite for material rewards. The awareness of having a free will also enters more strongly each year - further complicating the tussle between our ego's personal desires, the appeals of our deep-seated spiritual identity and our connections to the diverse needs of society.

How to live in the world but not of it - quickly becomes the drama that besets every person - with the inputs from the Soul are likened to sowing seeds in a field in which the soil is not always fertile or receptive. Yet, ever notice...the promptings of the Soul, although not always heeded, never stop. And then periodically - and sometimes suddenly - often when we least expect it - we feel a strong urge to not only heed but assert and fully honor this spiritual impulse. With such responses come the reminder of another realm, one that resides both within and outside of us, prompting us to concede Its role and thus do something about it. At times the impulse registers with such depth and expansiveness that we naturally lose sense of the ordinary Me as we simultaneous welcome and fully embrace the profound immortal friend we know so well.

Spiritual Encounters

A word...a setting...an experience...could trigger the feeling, the awareness, the sound...that directly acknowledges contact with something otherworldly. It may appear as a glimpse into another domain. Soon it repeats Itself, has no immediate or apparent cause - lasts but a second or a full minute - then leaves as quickly. Such a deep sense of something beyond the ordinary has little to do with the dramas of everyday living yet they may be evoked by the most innocent of happenings. Yet they are each and all so powerful that they're difficult to forget – leaving you pondering, wondering, and at times totally overcome. You see something, feel something, hear something as if from another realm and then suddenly discover your body shaking.

Shaking your head, you might initially chalk the incident up to some silly quirk of the moment. 'Forget it' is your everyday conclusion – since there is no way 'it' made any sense. You think the tune-in or tune-out probably stemmed from the unconscious recesses of your mind, a delayed and distorted reflection of something you read in a book, heard on TV - or dreamt about after eating very late last night.

Still the experience is not easily willed away. You keep recalling how the it surprised and even startled you. And just yesterday - 'the latest one' sparked a recall of all the other times you were suddenly swept up into an apparent encounter with some other domain. Gradually you realize that although you may have dismissed or rationalized each individual experience as 'strange, out of this world and inexplicable', each new one - given its cumulative effect - stirs an everdeeper sense of resonance.

Finally, you allow yourself to accept the reality that there are not only great similarities between these individual glimpses but taken together they shake your innocent presumption that your existence is only three dimensional, that it unfolds within a stable universe and is solid, definable and certainly predicable.

So you begin to acknowledgement that the glimpses you've received of some 'other dimension' may indeed be true - even those in which you saw yourself and others wearing different costumes, living in different and even strange environment, even walking through a field or interacting with others in settings that seemed to come right out of a movie. Slowly - almost reluctantly - you admit that it is time to consider the possibility that you are really having insights into or involving some aspects of your soulfulness - perhaps even recalling other times your Soul seemingly incarnated.

There was the time, for example, when the word 'intergalactic' stirred your long-held interest in the star Arcturus, the constellation of Cassiopeia and the wondrous mysteries of Pheiades or 'the seven sisters'. You even sensed you 'knew' you have been to each. And, oh yes: there is that recurrent dream, the one in which you sensed yourself flying, the radiant blue earth on the horizon growing larger and larger as you – as an out-of-body Soul - was returning to your embodiment just as you hear the tinkling of bells or your alarm going off.

You take a mental inventory of these experiences and realize these snapshots of another you in - or of - another realm can reappear to you at any time, day or night. And they have been numerous and vivid enough that you can no longer ignore their testimony. They are you - intimations perhaps that your Soul is living other lives. Or perhaps they are depictions of you from earlier times - of one or more of your Soul's previous incarnations. Whatever they are, they surely are a commentary on what appears to be larger, deeper and immortal you, vivid hints indeed that you or some aspect of your immortal Soul - has existed at other times and even in other extra-terrestrial realms.

Review and Compare

You review and compare your notes on your cumulative experiences, read about and research some of the topics they raise, chat with sympathetic, trusted and spiritual friends, and begin to put the pieces together, realizing it is entirely possible that you – or some spiritual energy called your 'Soul' during any one or more of Its many incarnations - has indeed existed in other historical times and/or cosmic dimensions.

Despite your immediate preoccupation with your current and seemingly apparently only earthly identity, you now realize your roots may also be spiritual and that in addition to your current sense of being 'just' an everyday human being, you may very well be your Soul's latest in a long line of incarnates. Such a realization makes it clear that you - a soulful incarnate - are thus not only in partnership with The Divine but that you are in fact a part or reflection of divinity ITSelf.[22]

That realization can startle you. You have had your mini-glimpses but you have never realized anything this profound.

So your body may begin to sake...and you weep...reach for the side of a chair or table - overwhelmed by an acute awareness of your profound existence.

---

22 Through the ages, a series of would-be 'mystics' have proclaimed themselves to 'be God' - and were summarily dismissed or punished. Yet they were on to something. We incarnates surely are not God. We are very closely related to God, however. since our immortal Souls are indeed direct components, aspects or cells of the cosmic reality known as The Divine.

Slowly, you wipe your eyes, sit up, and resume regular breathing. Unsteady, you stumble to get up...periodically stopping to feel your body, pat your face and stretch your shoulders. You reach for cold water ... splash it on and over your face and head, then just sit still for a while, slowly regaining a sense of being back in 'the now'. Clutching the back of a chair, you begin to notice the pictures on the wall, then slowly awaken to the sounds of our neighbor's lawn mower. Instinctively you nod repeatedly, then bow - and with open hands... give thanks for becoming intensely aware of knowing you are more - so much more than you ever dreamed.

Now What?

Suppose you - the reader - have literally been at such a point: finally affirming you are more than you ever thought you were. Yet you also know you are still the same human being you have always been. It is just that things have happened to and within you lately that make you feel you are something deeper and more extensive than the everyday you, something even spiritual in nature.

So you stop to think, recall and take stock, asking yourself a series of questions you may have raised before but never fully explored.

You may have harbored a set of hunches for some time - extensions of what you can only describe as dreams, mini experiences and then even jarring encounters that suggested there was more going on in life than your normal set of sensations and activities.

Has it not dawned on you that the person you think you are is only a part of a larger scheme of reality, that your supposed clear and discernible definition of your personhood is only a segment of the enormity of the Life in which your everyday life is enveloped?

Surely you have become increasingly aware that the everyday you play a significant role in revealing your mystical reality, a pivotal role in helping you manifest that which can only be considered *sacred*. You may already have already that the opportunities to make the world a better place really are signals that you are on divine assignment - that you are in essence an ambassador of the Divine wrapped in human clothing.

Have you not been given – actually gifted with - experiences that lead you to affirm the everyday mortal-you is glorified - part of a much deeper identity known as an immortal Soul?

Surely you sense your deep, inner soulfulness is immoral - although it is embedded in the flesh and blood of a human being who is very moral and thus subject to decay and death.

Aha: do you not realize yet that the mortal person bearing your name and living at your address – exists for only a limited number of years yet carries within in it a message, a bearing, an assignment from your creator - that you - simultaneously are - an immortal Soul!

Has it not dawned on you that the wondrous human being you are - is but the temporary home for a much larger and more powerful being known as an immortal Soul?

If so, then surely you realize that it is the process of incarnation that enabled You to settle unto the earth, embody Itself as an incarnate that bears your human name, and set Itself on a path of supporting the intentions of The Lord. Have you not yet realized that *You* - and all the other billions of Souls infused into *their* respective human embodiments - have been placed on Earth in order to transform it with your portion divine love and compassion.

The Everyday Spiritual You

The everyday you is also the spiritual you, the mortal being and the immortal Soul are aspects of the same being. The human you gives physical support to the immortal Self or Soul within it. In action, Me and My Self are a unit, identical, one and the same.

In My case, William is moral, has played his role and so will eventually pass from the scene. I Aeneas, however, am immortal and thus will help to form another incarnate once, William, my current incarnate has passed. So be patient, dear Aeneas: bear with and thank the mind and body of your current incarnate - for they have helped to carry You on to the next phase of Your life everlasting.

Sooooo - as noted, it is quite possible that the mortal or human you has increasingly sensed the presence of the spiritual and immortal You - heard Its whispers, sensed Its presence, listened to Its beckoning, heeded It's invitations, followed Its and advice.

Remember: your inner Soul formed and has lived within the mani-fest-you since incarnation, and has since constantly sought to guide you in the ways of generosity and understanding.

Please know then that you are here for a reason.

Please know you have a role to play.

Please realize – if you haven't already - that the central transformative energies of the universe are *unconditional* love and compassion.

And please know that the blessings of the Lord are being bestowed on You continuously - in both visible and mysterious ways – every day and in every way.

You have also been empowered to affirm and then share Your identity with others.

Whatever Your earthly focus, whatever the content of Your daily involvements, You, as an aspect of God, are entitled and expected to model the ways of the angels as you act to attain your earthly and heavenly goals.

As you assume any number of roles throughout your mortal life - an accountant, a student of art, a musician, a businessman, a waitress, an architect, a parent - wherever your talents and interests take you, be sure to affirm both the blessedness of your human nature as well as your divine or soulful identity. Even in the face of difficulties, the everyday person who knows they come from soulful roots is inclined to handle and resolve such outer differences for in doing so they in essence thus honor everyone's common spiritual roots and soulful identity.

This means that all the people who come into Your life are likely to be the very people who will help you learn how to face the challenges and make the kinds of contributions you agreed to before being birthed into this earthly domain. Even that ornery person you met at the supermarket the other day, and that guy who seemed to cut you off on the highway, may have been playing a role that forced you to slow down and heed the needs of others. Without both the annoying and the supportive presence of others, none of us learns how to grow in the depth and extent intended and needed.

Besides, if everything is easy, peaceful and predictable, and you are not fortunate enough to 'rub' against both irritating and kindred Souls, this lifetime or incarnation may be stripped of any opportunities to grow and develop. Just humming along may feel fine at the moment but it gets to be mighty boring, lifeless and of little consequence in furthering your intended spiritual growth and development.

There are no guarantees, for course, that you will realize or optimize your potential - for as much as your inner and creative Soul prompts the everyday-you to follow in the ways of The Lord, you are now and always will be a free agent. Despite the temptations to do otherwise, you know you must learn how to earn your way - choice by choice by choice - choosing what seems like the difficult way simply because you know it is the best way to support and perfect your spiritual essence.

You, the incarnate, the human being - are in essence the tip of your Soul's spiritual and cosmic spear. As You uncover and increasingly honor the revelation that inside the everyday 'you' is another wider, deeper presence - namely an immortal Soul - You realize that You are indeed the creative architect of your everyday profile and mission, the very caring hand that guides and nurtures every aspect of its and Your unified development.

Mere belief in the presence of your abiding Soul then is not sufficient to attain the spiritual goals for which you – the everyday identity or person - was fashioned. Spiritual realization involves a partnership where one aspect works with the other – where the individual and the Soul, the Me and the Self, the physical and the spiritual, the everyday and the everlasting, the immediate and the eternal - deliberately affirm their unity and act as One.

Chapter Two. The Formative Element:

The Immortal Soul Identity As '*My Self*'

Hello, My Name is Aeneas

HELLO. MY NAME IS AENEAS. I AM AN IMMORTAL SOUL. I HAVE manifest on Earth as a human being many, many times. At the moment, I am the Soul that first formed, was infused into and have now become the incarnate William. He and I are thus one and the same - two sides of the same unitive Being, one side mortal and the other immortal, the former manifesting its life in the everyday while the latter inspires that work with the love and energy of Heaven.

As a Soul, I am one of the gazillion cells or components of Prime Source. I am authorized and encouraged to utilize the process of incarnation to create embodiments of MySelf in the world of physical reality. As such, My incarnates or embodiments are intended to serve as ambassadors of The Lord wherever they are placed in the universe. They are in essence 'field agents' who communicate their experiences to The Lord while also being 'hard wired' to do whatever they can to foster love and compassion in the earthly domain.

Thus I, Aeneas - an integral aspect or component of The Divine Lord - helped to form the embodiment known as William. With the consent and support of The Lord, I chose William's main characteristics and arranged to have him placed him in a setting where he could best contribute to The Lord's goal of maximizing empathy, understanding and helping one another.

While still in the dormant and formative stage – William's emerging mind and heart agreed to the development of what were to be his main physical and emotional characteristics. If all was not right, at any stage of the maturation of his fetus, I - again with The Lord's permission - could adjust the process and concede the right of the mother to abort for any reason. [23]

My Identity

It is through incarnation that God in essence uses us to invest a portion of ITSelf in each incarnate, enabling ITs component Souls - Mine and Yours - to form and become unified with the mortal persons who are born and walk the Earth.

The otherwise transcendent God then is not only manifest in the visible universe through the perpetual presence of the twin aspects of the Master Soul, Yeshua and Mary. God is also present - and in fact is spread throughout in the physical world - in and through the billions of incarnates we Souls have helped to create. And it is when our incarnates finally come

---

23 Whatever the reason, an abortion is justified at the discretion of the pregnant woman simply because the fetus is not a person until the Soul enters into it - and that does not happen until the exact moment of a newborn's physical birth.

The need for an abortion is especially warranted if the woman was unwillingly impregnated (stemming from rape, incest or abuse), if her life was endangered by the pregnancy or potential delivery, if the fetus had become so diseased or damaged during the pregnancy that it was determined the newborn could not live a full life, or if the mother and/or her family is demonstrably unable to care for a newborn/child.

to realize who they really are - earthly reflections of the Soul-aspects of God ITSelf - that they are able to become truly alive and have profound spiritual impacts on the world! That means that you, the reader of this book - the incarnate of an immortal Soul - are also a part of God.

We Soul/incarnates are thus the creative force that sustain our version of The Sacred Trio - being the part of God that enabled ITs earth bound representative to act for It in the physical domain. Our everyday and mortal incarnates - like William and you - are The Lord's intermediaries that help IT to spiritualize the universe. How? By infusing Ourselves into Our incarnates we are able to transform what would otherwise be mere mortals into ambassadors of Prime Source - capable of using Our words and actions to generate ever deeper levels of love and compassion in the manifest world.

Dual Spirals

Astrophysicists confirm that as interstellar space continues to expand - with new galaxies and their sets of stars of planets appearing every day (or at least being discovered by our astronomers almost every day) - each one moving away from the millions of others at ever greater speeds. In fact, our awareness of the continual expansion of the outer cosmos corresponds to our insight into the depth of our souls and inner spiritual universe.

The universe seems to be is composed of twin spirals - one growing wider and higher with each iteration, and the other going deeper and more inclusive with each of its ever-widening arcs - best illustrated by the attached diagram of the double spiral. In spiritual terms, the double spiral shows how the growing expanse of the physical universe is progressing in line with the accelerating possibilities of our interior spiritualization, the inner always emulating the outer and vice versa.

We Souls - as infused into and appearing in the likes of your embodiments and mine - play crucial roles in establishing and sustaining the continued evolution of this outer-inner transformational process. It is our awareness of this dual-edged process that motivates us to align the depth of our everyday intentions with the demonstrable realities of the cosmos.

Each astrological discovery we make into understanding the nature of what astrologically is both beyond yet all around us, finds its complement in our growing insight into the depths of the human psyche that influences everything we do. Which aspect creates and reveals and which mirrors and mimics remains to be uncovered although they seem to play both alternating and simultaneous roles.

The Process

My particular external agent for My internal identity during this current lifetime on Earth, is, of course, *William.* Now 'William' may or may not always listen to Me - Aeneas, his immortal Soul - or abide by My advice - since he, like all incarnates in this physical world, is fully empowered to exercise his free will. So there is no guarantee that he will follow My soulful guidance. In fact, as we have noted throughout - it is possible that he will feel free to ignore or reject any one or number of My entries.

William, of course, is only the latest in a string of human beings that Prime Source has enabled me to create as We Souls help to fulfil ITs mission to further the cause of love and compassion throughout the physical realm.

In fact, you surely have realized at this juncture, that you - the reader - are a product of this process of incarnation – the sacred mission by which all immortal Souls – like yours - have charged corporeal entities like you with the responsibility to transform your immediate earthly environment in the name of love. In so doing, the 'mere' mortal or incarnate aspect of you is playing a crucial role in the ongoing transformation of the physical world.

Now this is a lot to absorb – especially given your Earth's long history of remarkable progress in science and ethics at the same time many of your citizens are producing a trail of devastation and cruelty. All Souls have been trained how to counsel their incarnates in the ways of love and compassion, and many have indeed succeeded in guiding many of their incarnates to become enlightened. Yet We Souls have only succeeded in part, for as many individuals and groups rise each year to support the urgings of Spirit, many have been thwarted by the politically and morally corrupt leaders who appear in almost every historical period.

Yet when viewed over centuries and even epochs, the signs of progress have been inescapable. Although they are still with us, fewer dictatorial regimes have emerged over time and when they do they rule over less expansive domains. The regimes of Genghis Khan are gone and the hideous regimes of Hitler and Stalin did not last very long. Pockets of fascism continue to rise and fall although their reigns have been greatly shortened and weakened. The long arc of history thus portends fewer lasting restrictions on the freedom of speech, assembly and spiritual expression, aided in good part by the spiritual intentions and actions of each new generation of incarnates.

In recent years, for example, incredible progress has been made in affirming the rights of women and minorities. And surely the ignorance that once dominated the medical field - such as extensive bleeding and half-baked concoctions - has been replaced by the discovery of treatments and cures for almost every part of the body and mind. Modern medicine - although still lacking a cure-all for all our bodily and mental difficulties - is the product of centuries of ingenuity and insight. In the same way, structured buildings have fortunately replaced caves and huts, and the gradual emergence of musical instruments and orchestras have replaced the prior reliance on grunting, banging and the rubbing of sticks and stones together.

I realize I am brushing with very board strokes, but the flow of history has for centuries been one of substantial progress in every major aspect of society. Slowly but inexorably, the unrelenting evolution of human consciousness championed by each set of increasingly progressive incarnates - has also produced an expanded recognition of love, equality and the virtues of individual freedom. War, degradation and devastation have certainly appeared and still exist. But over the ages a host of safeguards, treaties and declarations of the rights of humankind - and all Life - have greatly helped to civilize and uplift society. Problems and deviations have continued to emerge but they are also being judged by higher and higher standards.

Admiration

Now that I - Aeneas - have gone public and entered into the fray 'in person' so to speak, it is hard not to add My admiration for all the efforts that have honored such higher and deeper standards of belief and behavior.

The Lord's mission has not been fully realized but progress has been registered - and it continues. The reins to the Lord's great chariot depicted in Tarot card number seven, for example, are now being deliberately espoused by significant portions of society. The blessings and invitations of the Spirit - manifest in diverse forms yet displaying a common core - are now central to the missions and manifestations of an ever-increasing set of truly soul-abiding incarnates and organizations.

We know all too well that intense forces of resistance also continue to emerge, but the empowerments of the wise, despite suffering setbacks, have continued to expand. More and more people seem to accept their personal responsibility to support the loving transformation of the earth with ever greater vigor. It is what I urge and support for William. I know many, many immortal Souls are taking the same stance - living up to their status, role and mission - offering Their encouragement and support to each set of incoming incarnates.

The Transfer

What exactly does it mean to be a Soul – a facet of the eternal Divine, a cell in a cosmic organism? To be part and parcel of The Divine is undoubtedly a position of empowerment - including the responsibility to use the process of incarnation to help our Lord manifest ITs spiritual intentions in the realm of everyday living.

Will that goal ever be completely achieved – given each incarnates capacity to also exercise free will? Progress is being made with each passing year - with spiritual heroes and heroines emerging in each era to spur on the activities of the general population. The continuation of such progress depends how we each answer a set of crucial questions:

How long have We Souls toiled? It seems like forever and that is exactly right, that is since our creation by The Lord so many eons ago. And how effective have our string of incarnates been ever since? Is Your current incarnate ready and able to stand on their predecessors' shoulders and both solidify then continue to support the progress they made in implanting their commitment to love and commitment? In fact, how great is Your current incarnate's sense of appreciation and thanksgiving for the contributions made by their predecessors?

Question: is the determination of Our current incarnates strong enough, and their sense of empowerment extensive enough, for them to overcome the negative forces of the Earth? And will their patience fade if We Souls don't do everything We can to fortify and guide them, thus helping them avoid serious bouts of compromise and sluggishness?

Are the actions of all Our current incarnates worthy enough to encourage The Lord to call for Us to incarnate one more fortified generation of volunteers? If so, will Our newcomers be able to bear the strain of everyday living and live up to their promises? By the way, how do We Souls and our embodiments ever know which of Our incarnates' actions are having the intended impact? Do We just trust that they do, or is there a discernible feedback system that encourages both Souls and their incarnates to 'keep on keeping on'?

Here We immortal Souls are producing spokesmen destined to be everyday citizens of the world, expecting that We together and work Our way through all the ins and outs, the twists and turns, the visions and disappointments of life in the material realm. Through it all, We learn to deal with a stream of both ordinary and very significant stuff – yet often do so unmindful of the fact that We empowered Souls need at the earthly level to act through our very vulnerable personas. As creative Souls embedded in material bodies, We are able to recall everything from an incarnates childhood - including the events of yesterday. We are equally apt to harken back to their - and thus Our - pre-birth spiritual promises. In fact, We can do the same for all of Our earlier incarnates although such cumulative memory is limited to what the three-dimensional mind of Our current incarnate can access through its meditations and dreams.

As noted earlier, such hints and clues of the activities of earlier incarnates can and do emerge during the first three years of each successive human incarnate. But that awareness fades throughout life as each incarnate increasingly focuses on such earthly experiences as schooling, vocational life, sex, and relationships.

Together

It is only in Our later or senior years as an incarnate that memories of Our earlier embodiments reemerge with any intensity. It is then that they become more fully aware of their Soul and thus divine identity. It is then that they are also reminded that mortal life is short and that We together - body, mind and Soul - had best act in synch, shore up our spiritual intentions and make a series of conscious contributions to the welfare of our neighbors, kinsmen and society. It is through regular monitoring, meditating and prayer that the incarnate self receives greater and greater insight into its spiritual heritage and responsibilities.

Given the demands and enticements of earthly living, however, such reminders and encouragements have a very rough time breaking through to an incarnate's consciousness and actually spurring them on to action. With time and repetition, revelations do reawaken our mutual sense that 'We are - after all - originally and primarily immortal Souls'. Reminders and glimpses thus urge Us to persist - to say 'yes' to the invitation to encourage our mortal embodiments to affirm that they are merely a visible or grounded part of something more expansive, something much deeper, something in fact that is of utmost importance, to wit - we everyday folk really are *immortal Souls - celestial beings who* have taken on a human mind and body in order to become tangible expressions of The Lord.

And so We pray: May Our everyday embodied incarnates learn how to overcome each and all of their divisions, see and affirm themselves as aspects of God and come to realize that all their mortal experiences involve encounters with other deeply committed immortal Souls.

Close Although Far Away

The appearance of a newborn's head indicates the generic need to be born and push on. The ensuing yelp confirms the impulse to expand that energizes every phase of our continual unfolding. Miraculous as it may be, we still cannot fully understand the process by which a curious yet intentional sperm finds its way to its seemingly receptive mate. Surely it is an apt symbol of how and why incarnate humans continually seek to advance - in body, mind and soul - through the stages of childhood, youth, the teens, adulthood and seniority. Our ensuing development - with all its expanding visions and empowerments - including the recent James Webb telescope (launched on December 25, 2021) that can now survey the cosmos as it appeared only minutes or approximately 100 million years after the Big Bang erupted some 12.7 billions of years ago. Given the expanse of the universe since then, the Webb telescope can see the light from the Big Bang that now appears some 46 billion light years away. [24]

On the human scale, of course, it has been the mating of embryonic cells that set the stage for the unfolding of life. The cycles of life - from infant to adult - occur so gradually that they unfold outside our conscious awareness - seemingly so automatic that the process itself is unfathomable. Yet when any phase of any transition is closely monitored - becoming noticeable - it is witnessed with a deep sense of awe, thanksgiving and celebration.

Evolution and Visitation

That brings us to the beginning or unfolding of life on Earth, which at its most granular stage began some 4000 million years ago with the

---

24 See htts://webb.nasa.gov

emergence of what the scientists call 'sulfate respiring bacteria'. Note the measurements are noted in billions of years with the Big Bang occurring approximately 12.5 billion years ago, and the formation of the Earth some 3.5 billion years ago.

What a happened in between? Well in addition to the continuous unfolding of the physical cosmos into billions of galaxies, each with its billions of stars and planets, life emerged on Earth and perhaps on thousands of planets in other galaxies. Together our astronomers (who examine the history of outer space), paleobiologists (who study of living organisms), paleontologists (who study fossil remains) and geologists (who study the geological history of the Earth) have discovered that life - once present or created - evolved around our globe in a continuous stream of ever more complex forms. [25]

Thus the ensuing switch from billions to millions of years: pure or naked mitochondria emerged around 3000 million years ago, photo-syn-thesis around 3900 mya, fungi and proto-animals 1700 mya, plants approx- imately 1300 mya, sex 1000 mya (?), animals with vertebrate, 670 mya, elemental brains and nervous systems 620 mya - with life coming ashore around 425 mya.

Then Humanoids (almost human) like Australopithecus afarensis (literally apemen) did not appear until approximately 2 mya, followed by Homo habilis in 2.4 mya, Homo erectus (Lucy) in Ethiopia around 1.9 (mya). The appearance of Lucy was particularly notable because Lucy displayed hands for precise griping and the eating of meat. That same species mastered fire by 1.4 mya.

Following the migration from the tropics of Africa and the dispersal of the homo species into Europe and then Asia, the remains of Java Man revealed a brain size of 875 cubic centimeters. Brain size then increased to

---

25 See Nigel Calder, *Timescale : An Atlas of the Fourth Dimension* (New York: Viking, 1983), page 249.

1300 cubic meters with the discovery of Peking Man around 1.1mya. Following an approximate century of cultural fine-tuning of physical size and related mental development of the brain, a 'standstill' of approximately 1440 cm settled in around 45,000 thousand years ago with the advent of the fully constituted human sentient sentient beings (that's us today: those who are aware that we are aware).

Thus did the continual increase in the size of the physical size of the brain make way for the increasingly enhanced power of the human mind - developments that reflected the arrival of the waves of increasingly advanced and progressive extra-terrestrials on Earth. It was also the natural mating between the two that brought about the emergence of enhanced civilizations like Atlantis and Lemur, and all cultural and structural break-throughs described below in Chapter Four, The Blessed Alignment, "Energy Flows." [26]

Cosmic Energy

The human brain has surely evolved - in fact, it has changed substantially in size, weight and thus function and capability over the millennia. What accounts from such incredible and periodic upgrades?

Modern science attributes the evolution to adaption and natural selection. According to the experiences and insights of both ancient and modern mystics and spiritual adepts, however, we immortal Souls have progressively gained access to understandings not available to those who rely purely on scientific observation and other rational approaches. The most gifted among us have - for millennia - used their ingrained empowerments of intuition, prayer, mediation and contemplation to activate their extra-sensory spiritual awareness. We therefore perceive the universe as operating in ways that reveal and confirm the following:

---

26 Nigel Calder, Timescale : An Atlas of the Fourth Dimension (New York: Viking, 1983), "Human Origins", pp. 241-2.

(1) Each of Us is an incarnate being that has - again, for millennia - been formed by an immortal Soul, and as such possesses enormous insight and spiritual empowerments.

(2) We each have been gifted with the capacities inherent to being a component part of or cell in the cosmic essence of The Divine.

(3) Therefore we are capable of directly experiencing the revelations gifted to us from the spiritual or extra-sensory world (such as the many outlined throughout this manuscript).

(4) Our existence on Earth - and the rest of the universe - may thus be attributed to the loving unity created by the blend of three sources: Soul, body and mind.

> **A.** Again the process of incarnation has played the key role. Thus did The Lord enable the immortal Souls who responded to the divine wish to incarnate - and thereby enabling them to infuse a portion (ten percent) of Themselves into each newborn they sponsor.
>
> In each case, The Soul was infused just behind the heart of the newborn - which accounts for the heart becoming the symbol of love and the sacred life.
>
> **B.** On the other hand, the basic development our incarnate bodies have followed the evolutionary path developed by our ancestors - namely the one described by our planetary scientists (including each advancement in the evolution of humans or Humanoids, as outlined above).
>
> **C.** En route to full development, however, the minds of each generation of incarnates have been increasingly upgraded and inspired by the waves of extra-terrestrial beings who travelled to the Earth from throughout the cosmos (using the 'wormholes', of course).
>
> Such beings have thus mated with and counseled the native earthlings for millennia, their increased wisdom continually fortifying the human mind - especially in the early years. As noted, such enhanced wisdom accounted for the long list of incredible cultural breakthroughs and structural advances that have been made throughout the centuries.

In sum, we are all - in essence - creative combinations, our bodies traced to the original humanoids and 'Lucys' of Africa, our creativity and mindfulness to the progressive waves of advanced extra-terrestrials, and our innate connection to the Divine attained through the abiding presence of our immortal Souls.

(5) Given our heritage and soul-identity, each generation of incarnates has been able to attract and absorb the insights and testimonies of those Souls who have walked particularly close to The Lord and even encountered ITs twin Master Soul - Yeshua and Mary - directly. We thus are especially indebted to the unknown and unsung heroes of the early millennia, and thereafter to the contributions of such biblical figures as Enoch, Melchizedek, Elijah and Isaiah. Then there were the Apostles of Yeshua including John of Jerusalem and Mary Magdalene, and the many followers of Yeshua sand Mother Mary - such as Paul of Tarsus, Francis of Assisi, Theresa of Avila, Meister Eckhart and Hildegard of Bingen.

Other deeply spiritual advocates of the gospel of love include Ari Aurobindo, Kabir, Rumi, Boehme, William Law and dozens of free or unaffiliated souls from all faiths and cultures.

And among the tens if not hundreds of adepts who have shared important testimonies are the likes of Rudolf Otto and his *The Idea of the Holy;* and Evelyn Underhill and her masterful work, *Mysticism.* And both Michael Talbot in his *The Holographic Universe,* and David Wilcock and his *Awakening in a Dream* explore a range of extended realities.

Then there is the challenging world presented by Erich von Daniken in his *Chariots of the Gods;* the many testimonies of Dolores Cannon, including *The Convoluted Universe*; and Aldous Huxley's classic, T*he Perennial Philosophy.* Psychologist, Michael Newton, in turn, used deep hypnotism to elicit the spiritual experiences of his patients, telling their stories in his books, *Journey of the Souls* and *Destiny of the Souls.*

Please consider as well all 135 episodes of *Ancient Aliens* - broadcast over ten seasons on PBS television. Surely Joseph Campbell's magnificent T*he Hero With a Thousand Faces* and his four volumes of *The Masks of God* *are essential, as is* everything written by C.J. Jung, especially his *Psychology and Religion,* and *The Undiscovered Self.* [27]

Impact on Personhood

So, our next inquires focus on our most significant transition: the miracle that created our spiritual perspective and now enables us to manifest the sacred realm through Our everyday attitudes, words and actions. Does the Soul's dramatic entrance into Our respective embodiments at the exact time of Our physical delivery match the other astounding feats of Life - including the creation of the cosmos, the dynamics that govern the in speed of light and the unfolding of the perpetual Master Soul? Well, surely it does!

Indeed, the fact that the Heavens open wide and long enough to enable an invisible shaft of spiritual energy for Us to enter what then becomes 'Our' body at the exact moment of birth is miracle enough. But then to enable Us to continually nudge Our respective incarnations to fuller and deeper mental, emotional and spiritual development - a miracle that is reenacted world-wide every second of every day - is a remarkable spiritual achievement that belongs in its own category.

Talk about imponderables! Where do they end? We know so little about the exact workings of the Divine yet find Its presence in and guiding everything, beginning with the birthing process and continually unfolding as the moral compass of our lives.

---

27 My personal encounters with spiritual inspiration (aka guided or automatic writing) have been recorded in: *Trust Your Immoral Soul; Yeshua: The Continuing Presence of the Master Soul; The Return: Traveling With Mother Mary;* this current one, *Aeneas: The Biography of a Immortal Soul;* and the next volume - now in process and scheduled to be published in 2023: *The Wisdom of Archangel Gabriel.*

So we are indeed immortal Souls - heavenly beings now serving on what one television program refers to as 'the third rock from the sun" - a tiny dot spinning through space at the edge of one of the spiral arms of a comparatively minor galaxy. How indeed do We travel the astronomical distances involved - first in birthing, and now in completing the million and one tasks involved in fulfilling Our sacred missions?

Gateways

Our physicists now refer to 'wormholes' as our seemingly impossible 'cosmic highways' - gateways, dazzling interstellar tubes of light that operate like funnels, enabling anyone who enters one to gain 'immediate' access to any other portion or location of the universe. The term 'wormhole' refers to the channel by which we can transfer our bodily and spiritual energies across space. How it operates also gives us an important clue as to how We immortal Souls transport Ourselves from Heaven to Earth when We infuse Ourselves into Our respective newborns or incarnates.

As reported in the September 15, 1997, issue of *Scientific American*, for example, Professor Richard Mellon, a physics professor at Carnegie Mellon found that "wormholes are solutions to Einstein field equations for gravity that act as 'tunnels', connecting points in space-time in such a way that the trip in a wormhole [between otherwise distant points] could take much less time than the trip through normal space." The article includes multiple references to related research which suggest that instantaneous transport throughout space is not only possible but occurs frequently throughout the cosmos (presumably for angels, immortal Souls and beings from outer space who are aware of such powers).

Beings who utilize wormholes for intergalactic travel are able to travel to and instantly enter into another space that is geo or cosmo-graphically millions of light years away. The 'beam me up, Scotty' displayed on Earth's television's program, *Star Trek*, would seemingly be a unified force field that operates throughout the universe. For example, it would enable an immortal Soul to traverse any distance - including millions of light years of 'space' - from Heaven to Earth in an instant in order to embody Itself in a newborn incarnate. [28]

So does the seemingly impossible unfold, millions if not multiple billions of times a day - all over the globe, the planetary system, the galaxies and presumably the entire cosmos. Untold numbers of Souls who earlier 'today' had resided in the far realms of the universe, could very well be completing their journeys 'as we speak' and now be in the process of being displayed to their new human parents as an integral part of their newborn.

At the same 'time', millions of other Souls may well be traversing the outer reaches of the universe, instantly traveling to their intended destinations on one assignment or another. A given Soul, for example, residing on any one of the seven stars of say, Pleiades, could now be signaling to one of Its celestial cousins living on one of the stars in the belt of the constellation of Orion. The message: It was about to visit, suggesting they might meet on the giant planet, Arcturus, from whence they would transfer to another wormhole that would instantly funnel them to Hawaii for a well-deserved vacation.

OMGoodness

Just how far and fast would such entities have to travel - in a wormhole or not? We on Earth measure such travel in terms of light-years. Do the math: light travels at 186,000 miles a second, which times 60 seconds a minute equals 1,160,000 miles; multiple that sum by 60 minutes to an

---

28 According to Wikipedia, a light year - used to measure astronomical distances - is approximately six trillion miles or 5.88 to be exact, with the distance from Earth to most 'near-by' stars being measured in multiples of tens, hundreds and thousands of light years away. That puts the phenomena of wormholes and its capacity for 'instant travel' - no matter how astronomical the distance traveled - in an entirely new 'light'. See more below.

hour gives us 669,600,000 miles an hour; which times 24 hours in a day equals 160,689,600,000 miles. Then multiple that sum by 364.5 days in a year and the total of 5.8 trillion miles - in round numbers is equivalent to a yearly rate of approximately 6 to the 12th power, or 6 followed by 12 zeroes. Light therefore travels approximately 6,000,000,000,000 miles in one light year (give or take a few trillion miles).

Yet many of the stars in our own Milky Way galaxy are multiple hundreds, thousands and even millions of light years away. The Pleiades, for example, are only 444.2 light years away from Earth while the distance to the three major star clusters that comprise Orion's Belt – Alnitak, Ainiam and Mintaka - are respectively 1,260, 2,000 and 2,210 light years away. So a given Soul living in a 'heavenly state' on or anywhere near any of these star clusters could – with the help of a wormhole or two - embed itself in Its emerging incarnate on Earth in the relatively quick blink of the new-born's eye. The immediacy of such travel would also enable any fully formed person to traverse any distance in the solar and presumably even the cosmic system in an astronomical 'flash'.

For context, realize that most of the billions of galaxies in the cosmos are millions if not billions of lights years from Earth, so far away from us that our telescopes - even our latest ones - can only gain a faint glimpse of them, or sense their presence given their apparent impact on nearby formations. Consider - as well - that astronomers tell us that the farther away a star system or galaxy is from Earth, the faster is it moving away from us - a reflection of the continuous physical expansion of the cosmos.

It is right to assume then that any Soul on Earth is able to visit any other place or Soul in the cosmos It chooses, especially in the evening when the Soul is able to temporarily relinquish ties to Its sleeping and thus unconscious embodiment. That means a Soul could very well visit anyone, living anywhere - especially if It thought it could be of assistance: healing, advising, consoling and/or just sharing good cheer with old and new soul mates. Depending on one's motivation and/or response to a nudging from on High, the visitation list could also include one's original birthplace, family, friends and mentors, or the desire to learn something in particular while simply exploring new vistas.

Taking the Express

"Greetings to each and all of my Soul brothers and sisters: I just returned back to my original celestial home again - where I will stay - at a minimum - for what My Earthly friends call '24 hours'," cried a typical Soul. "I love the powers given us by Divinity that make it possible for We Souls to guide our particular embodiments throughout the day - especially when they are in distress or need extra counsel. But when they slumber - for a nap or especially at night when they may be bent on getting eight hours of sleep - I am motivated to join in or assist any and all - on Earth or throughout the universe."

"Fortunately, there is always one wormhole or another available to help Me reach My nightly destinations. It is also in My spiritual DNA to check in - as frequently as possible - with those in need any where on the Earth and even the galaxy. And as time allows - usually when My given incarnate turns on the 'slumber button' and simply decides to sleep some more - I also love spending time with my original family and close friends - reminiscing or just sharing. We all need that camaraderie wherever we are placed."

"I hope my sudden reappearance with you on Pleiades tonight has not startled you. This new express from Earth directly to my old neighborhood is such a wonderful addition – enabling Me to traverse the distance in a virtual instant - or in just a few seconds if there's a lot of intersecting traffic."

"As an immortal Soul, I - through my latest incarnate - I have also loved being a part of the happenings on Earth again – despite its climate difficulties, incessant political disruptions and some of the universe's most corrupt and self-centered beings."

"At least My present incarnate on Earth can now see and admire the Pleiades each night – as Our constellation slowly comes into view each spring in the Earth's northern hemisphere. Now that I am back – at least for a while - I realize again how dazzling our cluster of Seven-Plus Sister stars is and how easy it is for its array of bright stars to be seen from My current residence on Earth - given the fact that we are now situated on the comparatively faint Orion arm of the Milky Way."

Troubled Souls

"By the way, I have informed 'the Boss' of my traveling plans around the galaxy, and also received ITs continued and enthusiastic support for My travels to the many troubled spots here on Earth and - as needed - elsewhere. As you may know, the earthly plane continues to need all the guidance it can get - since it continues to harbor too many incarnates possessed by the so-called glories of violence and greed."

"Their wining maneuvers - as motivated by pure avarice, sloth and envy - continue to produce waves of fear, disease and dislocation - all of which has now motivated Mother Earth to periodically cleanse the many diseased domains that were so badly damaged by past power plays and wars. Unfortunately, the deep cleansing needed has necessitated the use of fire and flooding by Gaia [29] in order to destruct the poison that has seeped into the crevices of the earth. It no surprise then that the Earth - in order to regain its health - will have to undergo a series of cleansing calamities in the coming years."

"Many of Us have received mandates from the Divine to invoke an abundance of new incarnates capable of overcoming the temptations that corrupted and doomed many of their predecessors. If there is any group that can help Our Lord attain ITs continuing desire to spiritualize the

---

29 In Greek mythology, Gaia is the Mother of all Life and thus the personification of Earth. See James Lovelock and his Gaia Hypothesis as presented in his book, *Gaia: A New Look at Life on Earth*, which views the Earth as a self-regulating organism.

Earth, and Gaia's need to cleanse itself, then this current and very progressive group is it."

"So, I am pleased to be among those Souls now displaying a very positive outlook - cheering for each new crop of incarnates as one does for their favorite sports team. By fusing with and becoming each new set of incarnates, We intend to help The Lord - and our local Gaia - sow more unconditional love and forgiveness into all the physical arenas."

"We are also cheered on by Divinity's recent decision to reveal the appearance of a New or Second Earth. Many of our current Earth's most spiritually informed citizens will soon be transported to the new domain where they will have earned the right to exercise their greatly upgraded consciousness of the Fifth Dimension. More on this wondrous development when We speak next" [30] as noted below.

Meanwhile

"Excuse me for a moment: The incarnate part of me, namely William, is stirring and I need to stop My out-of-body travels and return to My embodiment. It serves Me well - although It is frequently discouraged by the unrelenting turmoil of earthly living. William's system - as an integrated mind, heart and body - has now served Me for more than eighty-six Earthly years and thus has earned the mantra – implicit in his realistic lament: 'there are too many body parts'. As is true for the aging process of all Earthly incarnates, as soon as one bodily difficulty is taken care of, another joins the woeful list and signals that it too needs some TLC and/or medical attention."

"As an immortal Soul, I am ever so appreciative of the fact that We Souls - despite aspects of Our soulfulness being installed or embodied in Our Incarnations - continue to live in Our natural disembodied state in

---

30 See below - Chapter Three, The Causative Element: 'Difficulties Ahead', and Chapter Four, The Blessed Alignment, 'The Second Earth'.

what Earthlings call *Heaven*. That innate part of Us - actually Our Essence - of course never has to worry about bodily aches and malfunctions because We don't have corporeal bodies - or wings either! When We form and become embodied in an earthly incarnation, however - in order to serve the loving intentions of The Lord - We naturally get to share fully in *their* experiences - making them, of course, Our experiences as well. It must sound complicated to you earthlings - but to We Spirits, it is oh so natural to be - as noted - *both sides of one united coin.*"

"But, I confess, there are times when this Soul does grow weary of forming one more incarnate for a world that despite all its God-loving and beautiful beings continues to get in trouble - usually because of devious incarnates who seek only self-advancement and power versus serving God and the best interest of the community. So We persist to do Our duty, helping as best We can, mindful of the progress that is made - slowly perhaps - but progress nonetheless. So long as there is a loving God - which, of course, is forever and ever!! - We shall continue to form, guide and support Our Lord and Life - in and through Our incarnate sides."

"Fortunately, I do not have any misgiving regarding My current incarnate. We are literally joined 'at the hip' and in the course of his life, We have developed full confidence in his devotion, stamina and ability to make the kind of contributions that do indeed please The Lord. In short, I really love being an immortal Soul and have the privilege of *hanging around so closely* with what fortunately has turned out to be a long line of dedicated and loving individuals. By working together, We have helped The Lord make the kinds of contributions to the material domain IT desires and it deserves."

"So that's it for now. I guess I just wanted to chat with My intergalactic friends and family. Despite My periodic misgiving, I really do love being an immortal Soul - given the many opportunities We have to appear in so many fascinating places as so many wonderful personalities. Serving on Earth in particular, although often a difficult challenge - makes it special for We know we are helping millions of our incarnates to 'earn their stripes' as they make their unique contributions."

"And now and for the next few years, We will experience the joy of helping millions of Our current incarnates make the transit they have earned - namely to the enlightened consciousness of Earth II! Wow! Stay tuned. More on these transits will be shared very soon!"

"In short: Who has a more exciting and gratifying role to play in Our incredible universe - than Us?! It even beats just hanging around the glories of Heaven."

"So: that's it for now. Watch for My interplanetary whispers, hints, invitations, e-mails, texts and visits. Either way I look forward to staying in touch - forever, of course - whenever and wherever Our ceaseless developments and 'wormholes' take Us."

With great love and appreciation to you and The Lord,

[Signed]: Your devoted friend: *Aeneas*

Summing Up

The bottom line: *I, Aeneas, do not have a Soul.* **I am a Soul.**

I am an immortal being and an integral component of The Divine Being who formed and continuously creates and recreates the cosmos.

The Lord has empowered Us to use the process of incarnation to serially form embodiments in the material world, infuse Our soulfulness into them and thereafter seek to guide them as their resident conscience.

My latest incarnate, William - like all who have proceeded him - is fully equipped with all emotional, physical, mental and spiritual empowerment's he needs to serve The Lord throughout his - and thus My most recent tenure on Earth - all to the end of fostering the adoption of love and compassion wherever I and My embodiments are placed.

As the immortal Soul of the incarnate author named *Shakespeare* once reminded all of Us:

All the world's a stage,

And all [Our] men and women [incarnates] merely players;

They have their exits and entrances,

And one [person] in his [or her] time plays many parts,

[Their] acts being seven ages." [31]

Thus, all of My set of incarnates - like Yours - have appeared historically in many guises. William is among those who are true – for he has always tried to live up to his contract and extend Divinity's loving essence into his varied involvements with and on the Earth. As you will see shortly, not all of My earlier incarnates - over the centuries - have done as well. They include some the world has deemed ruffians, nay-do-wells and scoundrels - while others have not only met expectations and fulfilled their promises but have even exceeding My – and, I sense, The Lord's - wildest expectations."

Recognitions

So we must deal with a stark reality: each of us here on Earth - at this moment - is an immortal Soul manifest in incarnate form. This time, I, Aeneas, appear on Earth in and through the incarnation of one named, William. Like all incarnates, he possesses certain abilities and faces a series of challenges. He is also both encouraged and bounded by the promises he made prior to its his incarnation. But his incarnation was and still is an open-ended adventure. He has now advanced to the point that he is now very conscious of the fact that he - like everyone else on Earth - is a temporary representative of an immortal Soul such as Me and You.

Unbelievable perhaps, hard to fathom – but true! I, the immortal Soul, Aeneas - have, in using The Lord's process of incarnation - helped to invoke William's appearance on Earth and am now guiding him in presenting this account of his spiritual experience. Therefore - and I cannot say it often enough: I, Aeneas, am an immortal Soul, a cell or component of Prime Source ITSelf, a delegate of and in direct contact with the Being that is

---

31 Shakespeare, *As You Like It,* Act 2, Scene 7, lines 139-143.

responsible for creating everything - including Me, You and Our centuries of incarnates.

Hmmmmmmm!

Earlier Incarnates

Sorry to say - as noted - that My list of earlier incarnations has presented a mixed bag. Some - in fact, many My incarnates have clearly been spiritual, kind, understanding, living up and in some cases exceeding the promises made prior to their formal incarnation. Some have even startled Me and gone on to play prominent roles in the history of earthly spirituality. Yet some others have been unsavory to the core, devious and made few if any contributions to the annals of love and compassion. The latter group, however, did help to fill in My profile, enabling Me to become personally acquainted with the broad range of personalities.

Even some of My less knighted incarnates made occasional contributions to spirituality even when they did not have the stamina or fortitude to act as I had hoped. Their shortcomings, however, might very well be attributed to Our combined needs to experience - and thereafter empathize with and forgive - a wide range of bland and decidedly unpleasant personalities We otherwise might never be aware of, and certainly not experience.

Realize, as well: each of Our earlier incarnates lived and worked within a context now centuries and millennia old – settings that were very different from those of twenty-first century. Yet they surely faced analogous issues and decisions – especially those involving the eternal struggle between the temptation to indulge the ego and the equally incessant invitation to affirm the presence and priorities of The Lord.

I hasten to add that each of the varied personalities I adopted through the centuries - no matter how outwardly disreputable some may have appeared - have helped Me understand why events unfold on Earth as they do. In particular, the fact that many of My incarnates failed to live up to their promises have thus helped Me, their sponsoring Soul, to recognize the limits of My Soul's powers, empathize more closely with the varieties of the human condition and forgive the vulnerabilities of those who never did learn how to model true spiritual behavior.

On the other hand, having multiple opportunities to see how many of My incarnates chose - despite very demanding circumstances - to be loving and compassionate, have encouraged Me to persist in helping every one of them to become more sensitive to their fellow 'inmates', especially with those who apparently signed on for - and subsequently endured - some very difficult assignments and situations.

Blessings and Temptations

Basically, however, I doubt if any of My brethren have ever felt anything less than fortunate for having been 'born' into or been placed in the earthly realm. Despite its pitfalls and temptations, the material realm offers a vast array of opportunities for every immortal Soul to recognize that many of Its incarnate forms have served The Lord in very specific and monumental ways: enabling The Lord to obtain firsthand knowledge of every conceivable human experience as they simultaneously enhanced the spiritual consciousness of the Earth and thus the cosmos.

Service rendered on the Earth, after all, is known to be both one of the most demanding and potentially the most rewarding placements in the universe. To find out, however, each sponsoring Soul has to incarnate anew and hope their steerage produces the best results.

You are now aware that you are in fact both sides of a wondrous coin - an immortal Soul who is responding to this story with full recognition of your spiritual roots as well as an everyday incarnate who has long sensed it does indeed have deep ties to the spiritual domain. In fact, both sides may be in the process of 'going public' with the news of your true or amalgamated identity. If so, going public - affirming your double-sided spiritual identity at least to just your trusted friends and family - is a fearful enterprise that can be both cathartic and affirming. Many an adept has discovered, however, that the most difficult 'audience' can be one's own family and 'old' friendships. They have always known you for your outer or demonstrable characteristics and now you claim to have experienced a deep inner spiritual dimension as well. Hmmmmm.

The experience of incarnating on Earth is always intense for the Soul. It is no wonder that being embodied on Earth is experienced with both exhilaration and trepidation, generating a sense that you have stepped off a well-constructed and revered golden spiral staircase onto what is very mushy ground one day before converting into a long, thin, rickety tight-rope by the weekend.

On the one side is the gratification of knowing you are empowered to love The Lord and ITs many incarnates 'now' and in person. On the other side, however, is the danger of not being able to withstand the storms associated with everyday living, even succumbing to one of its numerous temptations and – heaven forbid - tumbling into a life of selfish pursuits of power and material gain.

Twenty Thousand Incarnates

Some of the names of My many earlier incarnates came to Me during meditation. Others arrived as intuitive bolts of awareness. For example, I became aware of the ancient prophet Amos when his name arrived out of nowhere as a repeated whisper as I was waiting for a plane in a crowded airport.

The identity of others just popped into recognition or were triggered by something I repeatedly heard on radio or television. Others literally 'jumped off the page' when I would frequently come across their names while reading. Still others arrived insistently as I was sleeping - motivating Me to awaken and write their names down before I forgot. All of them have been confirmed by Benu.

Archangel Gabriel also suggested a few others during the over one hundred hour-long dialogues I had with Him over the last forty years. All of it was always accomplished through the mediumship of Karen Cook of

Albuquerque. [32] It was Gabriel who confirmed that My Soul has incarnated over twenty thousand times.

As noted, many of My earlier incarnates did not develop into society's most notable citizens. Gabriel confirmed that as well, although neither of Us was particularly interested in recalling their names or their involvement in various of egotistic and devious behaviors. As you will see, I am proud, however, of My many soulful incarnates who apparently did serve The Lord well and contribute to the spiritual welfare of society.

Be Aware

Perhaps you are already aware of the names of at least some of the earlier incarnate personalities your Soul has sponsored and assumed over the years. The names of others may come to mind as we proceed. If not, then ask in meditation to be enlightened. Be particularly receptive - in general and especially now as we proceed - to any insights and personalities that appear to you in your dreams, readings and reveries. Attend particularly to those names that just feel right, that appear repeatedly, that jolt you, that stir or reawaken a deep sense of recognition and resonance.

As in all things worth knowing - the process of recalling Your earlier identities may involve simply trusting in yourself and generating a joyful sense of adventure, expectation and appreciation. You are after all communicating with your most sacred sources of inspiration: The Lord, your immortal Soul, your current incarnate's Guardian Angel and your

---

32 Gabriel always used the name, 'Benu' during our readings. It is an Egyptian term meaning 'opening' and 'guide', adopted perhaps in order to relax those who might otherwise hesitate to speak directly to such a revered figure as an 'Archangel' - no less 'Gabriel', reputed to be the first Archangel created by Spirit.

Karen Cook retired from her work as a medium to Gabriel in July, 2022. It has not yet been revealed who - if anyone - will serve as the next medium to Gabriel.

confidence in your own spiritual and soulful identity. You need not to work at it. Relax, confident and thankful that you are now committed to 'listening' to the deepest recesses of our own spiritual being - allowing the messages to unfold ... spontaneously and with deep appreciation.

My Predecessors

The names of some of Our preceding incarnates absolutely stunned William as they were gradually revealed to him. Many of the revelations obviously seemed incredibly audacious. [33] "Me?" he would say. "My Soul was him or her in an earlier incarnation? You have got to be kidding?' That is hard to believe."

After days, weeks and even months, when the names of his Soul's earlier identities were confirmed and reconfirmed, he learned to accept his Soul's heritage - yet muttering 'wow', 'incredible' and an 'oh-my-oh-my oh my'. He has simply learned to accept his temporary identity as the current and thus temporary embodiment of his immortal Soul, having been preceded by thousands of other temporary embodiments. "This how Life works," he finally admitted. "It is how the spiritual world operates."

So as the current incarnate, William assures us that he still has breakfast every day, does his age appropriate (86) exercises every day, and completes his conscious and automatic writings every day. Although he continues to find it ever so incredible, he also finds it comforting to know he has been formed by the immortal Soul, Aeneas, and that it is through Aeneas that he shares in His heritage and thus The Lord's divine essence.

William also realizes that he is a member a spiritual group, and the names of all his predecessors were enshrined and registered in the base of his skull at the time of birth, and that his name will be added to that list

---

33 As you may have noticed that the word 'Me' is capitalized when it refers to Aeneas, the immortal Soul, but lower case is used when referring to His incarnate, William. The same is true, of course, for the pronouns 'My' and 'Us'.

when he dies. Such an honoring is a significant part of an incarnate's identity, knowing that their counsel is available to both the Soul and its latest incarnate whenever either invoke their essence.

As you can surely understand, whenever the specific name of a past incarnation is revealed and confirmed, it makes our united Soul-incarnate identity stop and take a deep breathe - bringing tears to Our eyes - invariably forcing Us to bow, open Our hands in thanksgiving - and re-experiencing Our connection to The Lord as a gift and a blessing.

Recurring Themes

There is a famous painting by Eugene Gauguin entitled: *"Where Do We Come From? What Are We? Where Are We Going?"* (1897-1898) [34] which continues to form a useful framework for exploring who we Really Are - and how We have manifested Ourselves in earlier incarnations.

In My case, as the Soul Aeneas, I start by reaffirming that I am an aspect of The Divine. I initially was formed in time immemorial and have always lived in the ethereal domain referred to on Earth as *Heaven*.

When expressed as an incarnate, however, I have borne the looks and empowerments of a human being and situated in the physical domain - usually *Earth*, which - as you know - is part of a sun-centered planetary system located on an offshoot of a major arm of the spiral galaxy called the Milky Way.

As will soon be revealed in the following pages, My Soul has assumed many different personalities over time - including the prehistoric, ancient, biblical and now modern periods. And each one has tended to unfold

---

34 See Debora Silverman, *Van Gogh and Gauguin: The Search for Sacred Art* (New York: Farrar, Straus and Giroux, 2000), Figure 170, p. 383. 'Dou Venons-Nous? Que Sommes-Nous? Ou Allons-Nous?, Museum of Fine Arts, Boston, MA.

around certain themes, the same ones that have continued to play significant roles in the life of My current incarnate, William.

These reoccurring themes have focused on one, spiritual identity; two, the capacity to convey healing energies to others; three, a tendency to question both civilian and religious authority; and four, the desire (and ability) to communicate one's experiences - in writing and the spoken word.

I have been told - again through William's conversations with Archangel Gabriel (Benu) - that I have invoked The Lord's process of incarnation to form over 20,000 incarnates. The exact number is unknown; the record of human embodiments since 'time immemorial' - that is since the evolution of sentient human beings some 150,000 years ago - are not available to Us at this time [35] - although the spiritual adepts of every age have claimed personal access to the full spiritual record detailed in the Akashic Records. [36]

Personal Meetings

A word or two regarding the process by which My current incarnate, William, consulted with Archangel Gabriel (Benu) - on any and everything - including the names and contributions of My earlier incarnates.

William [37] would make an appointment by telephone with Benu's intermediary, Karen Cook. She would answer at his assigned time, greet

---

35 See Nigel Calder, *Timescale: An Atlas of the Fourth Dimension* (New York: Viking, 1983).

36 The Akaskic Records are a compendium of everything that has ever happened. It is known as the spiritual book of records or the 'mind of God'. See Ervin Laszlo, *Science and the Akaskic Field: An Integral Theory of Everything (Rochester, Vermont: Inner Traditions, 2004).* The existence of such a record has also been affirmed by Rudolf Steiner and the spiritual-philosophic school of Anthroposophy.

37 Again, please be reminded that William and Aeneas, are really identical -

him - and after a few short exchanges would say: "Okay, I'll get Him for you (meaning Archangel Gabriel/Benu)".

William (or We) have also had personal, face-to-face appointments with Karen and been able not only to hear her initial greeting but witness her closing her eyes, moving her hand from her forehead to her shoulders, then bowing and then kissing her hand, after which she would literally slump over in her chair.

Within seconds, however, her body would sit up, assume a fully alert and 'spirited' position, and open her eyes. It was then that we would hear the strong and deep voice of Benu: "Greetings. How be you?" Gabriel had entered her body and the hour-long session had begun.

The ensuing conversation was easy and fluid, Benu in tone and language, encouraging Us to pose questions on everything from our perceived problems, plans for the future, and at some juncture, even - in this case - to comment on and verify the names of some of My prior incarnates.

So William, drawing on the names that had appeared to him in one way or another, would ask: "Did my Soul incarnate as him or her?" Or, "Was I in any way related to this person?" Invariably – as we will see – many of the characters named had indeed been one of My earlier incarnates and William predecessors.

Therefore

Many of those earlier incarnates were average citizens and did their best for their families, colleagues and neighbors. As noted, some surely were ne'er-do-wells - thieves, philanderers, vengeful warriors and thoroughly self-absorbed in manner and intent. Having gone rogue, they

---

one and the same - amalgamated when I, Aeneas, entered into the incarnation of William, the latest in the long list of the mortal beings I helped to form in order to express MySelf - and thus The Lord - directly in the mortal world.

apparently succumbed to one temptation after another and ended up ignoring many or all of the promises they made prior to their actual incarnation.

Yet I do not judge any of My earlier incarnates for failing to fulfill their agendas and participating in some lawless and degrading behaviors. Such missteps, frankly, may have helped Me as a Soul to attain a fuller understanding of the range and depths of the human condition - insights that caused Me to not only take greater care in safeguarding against such behavior but learning how to empathize and forgive it if and when it appeared in future incarnates.

On the other hand, there have been a number of My incarnates who appear to have turned out rather well, who in fact made loving and substantial contributions to the world's spiritual agenda as significant teachers and spiritual leaders - as well as family members, valued colleagues, students and friends of such adepts.

So here we go - with great humility noting the many fine incarnates I have had the pleasure to form and been associated with. Again, note how many of their activities clustered around the themes of spirituality, healing, questioning authority, and writing and communication.

One of My earliest incarnations was as Hermes, proclaimed an Olympian god in ancient Greece, herald of the gods and psychopomp or guide who conducted sponsoring Souls back to the heavenly domain following the death of one of their incarnates. Others included Asclepius, initially as the famed hero and god of medicine in Greek religion and mythology, the son of Apollo and Coronis, and father of such goddesses as Hygiene (cleanliness), Iaso (recuperation from illness), Aceso (the healing process), Aegle (overall good health), and Panacea (the energy of universal remedies for illness).

Asclepius' role in the Greek pantheon of gods was followed by his later manifestation as the renowned mortal and healer in the 5th Century BCE of Greece, the one who founded a series of healing centers, temples and sanctuaries throughout Greece including the famed one at Epidaurus.

A sculpture of his likeness shows him holding a healing rod entwined by a snake, the image now universally as the symbol of a physician's healing powers.

Gabriel has also told Me that I had also incarnated as a temple priest and served as a counsel to Akhenaten (reign c.1353-1336 BCE), the Egyptian pharaoh who abandoned Egypt's traditional belief in polytheism in favor of Atenism or the worship of the one divine, Aten. Apparently, I had also incarnated as a renown mystic and friend of Nefertari, the wife of Rameses II in approximately 1250 B.C.E.

Old and New Testaments

The linkage to spiritual leaders continued and was noted in various passages of the Old or Hebrew Testament. My Soul incarnated, for example, as a student of Elijah (ca. 900 BCE), the prophet who challenged the Temple authorities for their misdeeds, and even denounced local warlords who proclaimed themselves to divine and thus entitled to total deference.

I, Aeneas, also incarnated as a student of Amos from 754-746 BCE, helped him write *The Book of Amos* in the Hebrew Bible – and who today continues to serve as one of William's spiritual guides. The same is true with Ezekiel (ca. 600 BCE), whose prophetic work was outlined in the *Book of Ezekiel*. It was Ezekiel who prophesied the destruction of Jerusalem, the subsequent exile of the Jews to Babylon by King Nebuchadnezzar in 597 BCE, and the restoration of the Jews to Judah following that Babylonian captivity and the rebuilding of the Temple in Jerusalem in 537 BCE. Later one of My incarnates was an associate of Melchizedek, 'the priest of Most High" who praised and blessed Abraham (Gen. 14: 18-24; and NT Heb. 7:15-17).

Apparently, many of My most illustrious 'aliases' appeared in Jerusalem during the later biblical period - highlighted by the years I incarnated as a member of the Essenes and served with Yeshua in Qumran. Yeshua was then known as the *Enlightened One* and served as our leader in the years immediately preceding His being reincarnated later as the new born of Mother Mary. The future Mother Mary had also incarnated in Qumran as did the future scribe and teacher, Mary Magdalene. Both were children during the leadership of the Enlightened One.

A Long List

During the Biblical period on Earth, I was also embodied in and became the incarnate John, the son of Zebedee, the fisherman called by Christ while fishing in the Sea of Galilee (Matthew 4:21). John later joined the Sacred Family as they watched the mirage created by the laser-induced light-show - inducing many to think Yeshua had been crucified while in reality HE stood unharmed with rest of His entourage on a parapet over-looking the scene.

Thereafter, John traveled with Yeshua, Mother Mary, Magdalene and Joseph of Arimathea as they immediately left Jerusalem, traversed the Mediterranean Sea, traveled through Gaul and eventually landed in Britannia where they founded the Sanctuary in Glastonbury.

During this time, John took copious notes for what was to become the *Gospel According to John*. It advocated universal love and compassion and opposed the early Church's interest in adopting elaborate laws, prohibitions and structures that favored the rule of a self-professed hierarchies. [38]

Later I was embodied as Clement of Alexandria of Egypt in 180 A.D., the mystic who advocated for a free and personalized form of spirituality. My next incarnate became the famed Marcion of Sinope who maintained

---

38 See William Francis Sturner, *Yeshua: The Continuing Presence of the Master Soul* (Osprey, FL: Other Dimensions and Amazon, 2017); and *The Return: Traveling with Mother Mary* (Nokomis, Fl.: Universal Spirituality and Amazon, 2022).

that God spoke through the prophets and warned the Jewish people against the false claims of various warlords.

Serving the same cause, My later incarnates befriended and studied with Valentinus, the professed Gnostic- and then the pagan philosopher Libanius who lived during the last stages of the second century. A subsequent unnamed incarnate then became good friends with the brilliant Christian philosopher Origen, who by all accounts was one of the most influential and prolific theologians of the early Christian Church. [39]

In the interim, I apparently also incarnated as Augustine, the famed writer and theologian. Shortly thereafter My incarnate became a disciple of Pelagius, the Irish monk who opposed the doctrines of predestination and original sin espoused by Augustine and officially adopted by Church. Pelagius also upheld Yeshua's belief in the goodness of all human beings – views which were condemned as heretical by the Council of Ephesus in 431.

Benu also told William that one of My earlier incarnates was Arius (250-336 ACE), the cleric who emphasized the material nature of Yeshua – a perspective that helped subsequent generations affirm both Yeshua's incarnation as a Master Soul and the perpetual presence of Mother Mary on Earth following Her Assumption. [40]

---

39 False readings of Origen's many works alleged that he believed God the Father was superior to the Son (Arianism), denied a belief in hell and advocated universal salvation - which finally resulted in his being condemned by both the Emperor Justinian (543) and the ecumenical council of Constantinople (553).

40 Mother Mary was proclaimed 'the Mother of God' at the Council of Ephesus (461). Her Assumption enabled Her to join Yeshua as the combined female and male aspect of the Master Soul. It was not until 1950, however, that Her preeminent role was formally accepted by the Catholic Church, as defined by Pope Pius XII in his apostolic constitution 'Munificentissimus Deus'.

I was later infused into and became a few leading Europeans, beginning with Paracelus – the Swiss physician and alchemist who pioneered what became known as the 'medical revolution' of the 1500's. Paracelus emphasized the need for a thorough diagnosis, the prescription of medications tested in the laboratory, careful monitoring of each patient, the protection of wounds as well as the regulation of diet (replacing the earlier and exclusive use of bloodletting and the sewing up of wounds in plaster).

Thereafter I incarnated in a variety of roles including Fra Teofilo da Vairano, a colleague and dear friend of Giordano Bruno - the Dominican friar who was burned at the stake in Rome in 1600 for his advocacy of reincarnation, rejection of the doctrines of transubstantiation and eternal damnation, and upholding the discoveries and insights of the Copernican Revolution.

Later, my incarnations were dominated by a turn to the literary, initially as Thomas Traherne, the 16th Century poet and philosopher; then the prolific, influential and esteemed philosopher and writer, Georg Friedrich Hegel (1770-1831); followed by William Ellery Channing, the famed transcendentalist poet of Concord, Massachusetts (1818-1901); and then a close friend and confidante of such immortal writers as Walt Whitman (1819-1892), the naturalist Thoreau (1817-1862), and the transcendentalist philosopher, Ralph Waldo Emerson (1803-1882).

And lo and behold My Soul also appeared as Charles Williams, colleague of Tolkien and C.S. Lewis and one of the leading lights of the Inkings of Oxford University. He authored several very popular books during the very trying years of World War I that explored the mysterious workings of various 'spirits' in the lives of his characters.

Among my earlier incarnations – again as verified by Benu (Archangel Gabriel) – there was also Gerhard Jung, the brother and confident of Carl Jung, the revered Swiss psychiatrist and writer. [41]

Fulfilling the Sacred Trio

We thus have moved closer to the filling in many of the specifics that make up the sacred triad. In ascending order - you may recall - they are first, the person you and I know as 'me' - the everyday embodiment or incarnate who lives and deals with the daily issues of earthly life.

Then there is our true identity - namely the immortal Soul or the Self which formed you as Its current incarnate.

Now for the piece de resistance, the ultimate creator and the cause of it all, the third and all-inclusive portion of Our trio: the cosmic entity the universe knows as The Divine, aka The Lord, Spirit, IT or ITSelf, the Eternal I or Prime Source.

---

41 A few years ago, during one of my readings with Archangel Gabriel, He/It agreed that Carl Jung came as close as any human to understanding the relationship between the human spirit and the supernatural dimensions of the collective unconscious, or to what is referred to here as 'each and all of Us being a unity of earth and heaven, body/mind and spirit, incarnate and Soul - and thus everyday representatives and innate components of God'.

Chapter Three. The Causative Element:

The Divine Manifest As the Master Soul

PRIME SOURCE HAS WILLED TO INVOLVE ITSELF IN THE AFFAIRS of the physical or material domain - in other words, manifesting ITs transcendent or other-worldly, heavenly Self into a reality that can be experienced in and by the everyday world of materiality. Once infused into the physical domain, IT can thus empower ITs component Souls to incarnate and become daily advocates for divine love and compassion.

The result: the spiritual triad of mortal beings, immortal Souls and The Divine are incessantly working together to transform the everyday world into a reflection of heavenly values. Each of us now on Earth - and those continually arriving - have been formed by our respective Souls in order to fulfill the missions we agreed to at the time of our incarnation. It is clear each of us was incarnated here on Earth in order to complete the work originally inspired by The Lord, and then made operational by our Soul. We complete the Sacred Trio by being those who intend to physically implement divine purpose and intent.

Fabric of Life

To put it another way, The Sacred Trio - the unity of *Me, My Soul and The Lord* – *epitomizes the* fabric of life and is the source, the energizer and the immediate agent of divinity's creative genius. All three aspects are in alignment and work in perfect accord with each other, capable of converting that which is willed at the Divine level, empowered by soulful energy and carried into the limelight of created reality by the likes of you and me. The Trio thus works from transcendence to immanence to manifestation.

Yet in working through our such responsibilities at the mundane level, we everyday incarnates can often find our duties, desires and powers sidelined or delayed, often derailed or blocked by the intricacies and temptations of earthly living. A young Soul, for example, may not be ready to effectively guide Its incarnate - not having acquired the depth of experience needed to successfully fulfill the responsibilities of an Oversoul.

Even Souls returning from one incarnation after another often need more time and debriefing between stints to absorb the learnings and lessons of Their last placement. Some Souls may even need to be sidelined by The Lord if they show signs of having become lazy, uncommitted or simply unable to develop the depth of skills needed to successfully guide their incarnates.

Temptations Galore

Any given Soul - despite being a component part or cell in the cosmic body of Prime Source - may lose Its way upon incarnating in the earthly domain; we all know how easy it is to become enamored by the joys - and temptations - of incarnate life. As Soul-incarnates, we are always free to exercise Our free will and choose to ignore or undercut the urgings of Our resident Souls.

Rather than fulfill their best intentions, some incarnates may choose to procrastinate and even reject their Soul's counsel if they prefer to seek more immediate, material and egotistic rewards. Although trained and counseled in the ways of The Lord prior to incarnation, Souls may still lack the sufficient depth or repertoire needed to deal effectively with the complexities of earthly living, and thus be tempted to adopt attitudes and actions that undercut Their commitment to further the cause of unconditional love and compassion.

Souls and their incarnations alike have even been known to occasionally 'buck the system' - refusing to serve in places like the Earth - known for its very difficult sets of circumstances and challenges. Such reluctance is often overcome with additional counseling and retraining. If that does not work, a given Soul/incarnate may be asked to assume a less demanding assignment or simply asked to remain in the heavenly realm for more intensive counseling.

Such disconnects become especially evident when any given number of incarnates, in particular, become overly attentive to images of their own importance, choosing to fulfill the demands of 'selfish me' rather than respond to the prods and pokes of Their Souls and aspirations of The Lord. It is then that an incarnate would invariably sense intervention by their resident Soul - implanted as its conscience - poking at it with warnings that dangers lay ahead, even sounding the alarm to urge an incarnate to take the high and loving road or risk being recalled of left to its own devices.

Usually, the incarnate listens, but often it does not. If it strays too often and too far afield, it may totally lose its way, seriously undercutting the integrity of its personhood and even jeopardizing the honor and integrity of its resident Soul.

Nudges and Invitations

Nudges - whether from one's Soul, Guardian Angel or the Lord ITSelf - can certainly generate turnarounds or at least second guesses if an incarnate consistently heads in the wrong direction. Its typical internal dialogue: 'Is this really the right thing to do? Will I regret it? What could this lead to? Would I not feel more enlightened if I embraced a more loving or forgiving alternative? Have I not been created - and empowered - to serve The Lord and follow the promptings of My true and soulful identity?'

Such internal tussles can, of course, be settled by the call for 'Author-Author' - again pitting the incarnate-ego and its will free against its resident

Soul. Of course, the Soul, if invoked - given Its direct ties to The Lord or Chief Overlord - will ultimately win out - but if only the ego-incarnate relents and allows it. With prayer and meditation, the door to the Soul and thus The Lord, eventually swings open and little interventions provoke sudden awakenings. Messages, realizations - prompted by both internal and external stimuli - confirm the love and the will of Spirit – enabling incarnates like of you and me to heed the rustlings of our Souls - and realign with the impulse of our divine heritage.

Losing One's Way

Such realizations often break through as needed yet their effectiveness depends on Our ability to follow through with commitments and actions. Of course, a Soul could - as noted - also learn to tolerate and even vicariously enjoy the missteps of ITs incarnate, enabling It to look the other way, and thereby become a co-conspirator in Its incarnate's frivolous lifestyle - not only accepting but delighting in the degrading of Its true identity.

Such things do happen. Witness the long list of corrupt and hateful actions taken by an untold number of incarnate-Souls throughout the centuries. Corruption was also taken to extremes by the likes of the murderous Ghenghis Khans, the Hitlers, the Pol Pots, the Soviet Stalins, and the long list of crooks, outlaws and corrupt politicians who exemplify gross forms of ego-mania and depravity. In such cases, one can only ask: where were the Souls of these incarnates when their charges were perpetuating such tragedies? Some may have allowed Themselves to be brushed aside by the constant pressure while others may simply have succumbed to the temptation to go along and vicariously enjoy the ride.[42]

---

42 I include here the likes of Donald Trump, twice the impeached and America's perennially corrupt politician whose rejection of the results of the 2020 election has revealed his fascistic intentions - reminiscent of his previous

The continuing appearance of such compromised and degraded incarnate-Souls raises issues regarding the sacred nature of the incarnational process itself. Everyone - all incarnates - start out being formed by an immortal Soul and empowered to serve the imperatives of love and compassion. What happens when some Souls apparently allow their mortal creations to besmirch their training, ignore their promises and take actions that degrade any sense of decency, spirituality and humanity? Was the counsel of their consciences and the resident pleadings of their Souls totally ignored? Did leeway taken here and there - become license everywhere – creating a runaway ego seeking ever glorious victories with an ever-demanding sense of *me, me, me*? [43]

Inevitable Transformation

Alas, such lapses have unfolded throughout the history of humankind. But still the Lord, acting through ITs legion of truly enlightened Souls, has assured the constant replenishment of billions of loving incarnates. The Lord - acting through the vast majority of committed Souls - has championed the cause of the weak and the unfortunate, founded schools and philosophies of love and wholeness, adopted laws and activities that enhance the welfare of the family and the community, and spurred activities that encouraged millions of incarnate-Souls to find their way to their neighbor's door with a loving meal, and affirmations of thanksgiving, love and enduring friendship.

---

incarnation as Italy's former and very brutal dictator, Mussolini.

43 Surely this must raise issues in the mind of you, the reader, as to who you - today - experience as a renegade Soul-incarnate, a person who has lost his/her way, who has forfeited their identity as an integral component and representative of God and forsworn their commitment to think and act with love and compassion?

So it is that divine intent not only propagates the principles of love and compassion but helps ITs component Souls and their respective incarnates to ground ITs loving counsel in everyday attitudes and activities. Love and compassion apparently have never dominated every aspect of this planet or the physical universe. Yet despite the visible and too frequent appearance of rogues and corrupted Souls who choose to ignore their training and promises, the over-all process of spiritualizing the earth continues to gain ground - given the work and commitment of each batch of new incarnates.

In sum: the Sacred Trio is working ITs will - strengthening The Lord's commitment to a process of incarnation that encourages Souls and their embodiments to write with the indelible ink of love and forgiveness. From the cosmic - to the universal - to the everyday actions of ordinary but Soul enhanced individuals, the continuing success of the Trio is foretelling the ever-progressive transformation of Life – every day and in every way.

Difficulties Ahead

The road is likely to get rougher in the next few decades given the need for Gaia to cleanse itself of past devastations and continued neglect. Whether caused by war, greed or sheer stupidity, the see-no-evil, hear-no-evil and feel-no-evil attitude of many has devastated the land and corrupted the air and water resources of the planet.

So there are difficult decades ahead - making the dedication of loving Souls all the more essential. If the neglect continues to worsen, however, many Soul-incarnates may tire and simply choose to relocate to Earth II, the formation of which is just over the horizon.

If so, many who cause the devastation - through their actions or inactions - may face the consequences of their actions alone. Many of the more enlightened and dedicated Souls may simply decide to transfer to Earth II's greatly enhanced environment of 5th dimensional consciousness. More on these developments in the next chapter (Chapter Four) where We will focus on The Blessed Alignment with the untrammeled empowerments and The Lord.

Transcendent and Immanent

Let us first affirm the pre-eminence of the eternal and transcendent nature of the Divine (aka, Prime Source, God or The Lord). Then we will show how IT created and then revealed ITSelf in the immanent or physical domain - that is, manifesting ITs divine Self throughout the various eons, periods and cultures of history. The eternal has thus revealed the presence of the divine in and through the everyday life, the initial and ethereal other-worldliness of Prime Source reflecting ITSelf on Earth and entire physical realm as the perpetual presence of the Master Soul.

And that Master Soul has been revealed to us in and through the twin historical forms of Yeshua and Mary. Thus have the male and female aspects of the immanent God been placed on divine assignment - ready and able to guide us with divine wisdom - every day and in every way.

Prime Source, of course, remains the transcendental constant in the cosmic reality of divinity. IT is the sacred energy which preceded and then inspired the creation of the material or everyday world. As noted, IT then delegated ITs divine powers onto the Earth to the Master Soul, which - we will see - developed into Yeshua and Mary after many earthly incarnations.

Incarnation

The process of incarnation has thus played a crucial role in completing The Sacred Trio. God or Prime Source initially transmitted ITSelf into the immanent or physical world by first creating what is known in the Hebraic version of the Bible as *Adam and Eve*. God then sent the twin centers of the Master Soul from the ethereal or mythical realm of Spirit into the material realm of the everyday.

The Hebrew-Christian Bible describes their transit as an 'expulsion'. But their transit from the mythic to the everyday realm actually signaled the decision of the transcendent God to have ITs essence also be present in the immanent realm of the everyday. [44]

In Jungian psychological terms, the emergence of Adam and Eve as the initial versions of Yeshua and Mary, signaled that the archetypal realm of the collective unconscious was also being grounded in the concrete activities of everyday consciousness. As we will see, the God of the Heavens wished literally to reveal ITSelf as a concrete personality. Thus did Heaven ground ITSelf in human history - as subsequently recorded in such books as the Bible and the Koran. The once exclusively transcendent God was now also very, very active in the unfolding of our everyday world.

Once the twin aspects the Master Source were 'launched' - so to speak - on their journey to activate the fullness of their divine heritage, Prime Source directed ITs full attention to fully developing the process of incarnation. Cells or particles of ITSelf - as known here as immortal Souls - were also asked to make the transit to the physical ream, infuse Themselves into their incarnates - with the mission to propagate the essence God through acts of everyday love and kindness.

Both

So the likes of you and I became reflections of the cosmic and transcendent Prime Source, embodiments of our respective Souls and manifest as earthly personalities. What had been created eons ago in the ethereal aspects of Divinity was also to become immanent or ever-present in the everyday visible world. Our outer trappings as incarnates, however, were destined to last for but a lifetime; upon our demise, our immortal Souls are encouraged to form successors, who bearing their own characteristics - would pursue their own set of objectives.

---

44 See William F. Sturner, *The Creative Impulse: Celebrating Adam, Eve, Jung and Everyone* (Melbourne Beach, Florida: Helicon Press, 1998).

It was inevitable, then, that 'William' - like all incarnates - would sooner or later fade out or die and be replaced at some juncture by another incarnate commissioned by their respective Souls to advance their own agenda. It is not unusual that the agenda drawn up by each successive incarnate relate - in part if not whole - to the themes followed by earlier incarnates. And each incarnate gets to choose what and how it wishes to do God's work. As least, that is the plan when they - aka 'we' - form our intentions. As we have seen, however, not all incarnates - or their Souls - choose to abide by the promises and intentions they included in their pre-incarnational contracts.

The Unfolding of Yeshua

The immanent or physically manifest form of The Divine centers on the development of ITs Master Soul. As noted, true to ITs immersion in the material realm, the Master Soul evolved slowly over the eons of time. And true to the dualistic nature of that earthly domain, IT was manifest in ITs dual aspects as the male and female forms of Yeshua and Mary. Let's start with the development of Yeshua.

According to ancient records, the transcendent God first conceived of the possibility of manifesting ITSelf in everyday reality through an entity initially known as *Elder Brother* - who in turn evolved into *Amilius*. *Amilius was* apparently placed on Atlantis at the same time God created the angels - all in the hope they too would help to imprint ITs divine intentions on the created world. Many angels, however, chose to act like they were divinity unto themselves and began to approach the material realm with those bloated designs in mind.[45]

Amilius helped to reach settlements with the fallen souls and reestablish their ties to The Lord. But many rebelled again and again. Finally,

---

45 See Glenn Sanderfur, *Edgar Cayce's Past Lives of Jesus, op. cit., Chapters 2-16.*

Amilius pleaded with The Lord to allow Him - as a component part and extension of ITs divinity - to formally institute the developmental process of incarnation. The transcendental or other-worldly nature of the Lord would then (1) also become immanent or manifest in the physical realm through the slow but steady development of a Master Soul; and (2) God would simultaneously enable ITs component cells - or immortal Souls - to embody Themselves in the material domain as human incarnates.

Consequently, an early biblical Christian Nassene psalm reads as follows: "Then [the Master Soul] said Send us forth, O Father, therefore, and [we], bearing the seal shall descend and wander all Aeons through, all mysteries reveal. [We] shall manifest the forms [or component Souls] of the divine and teach the secrets of the holy way (enabling the Souls or forms of the divine to incarnate as earthly representatives)." [46]

Unity Splintered

It was through the recommendations of Amilius, then, that Prime Source decided to manifest or incarnate ITSelf in the material domain - an event that would over the eons and centuries culminate in ITs full manifestation as the Master Soul. Traditional religion tends to describe The Lord's extension into the realm of everyday living in biological terms, that is as His 'Son' with the connective 'blood line' or extension of ITs divine energy to be experienced as the 'Holy Spirit'.

Thus the transcendent unity of God in Heaven was divided into pairs or opposites to fit the bifurcated experience of the created world - such as hot and cold, high and low, up and down, here and there and so on. The normal unity of the Prime Source in Heaven or the transcendental universe would therefore be present in the created or immanent realm as the Master Soul - thus evident in ITs bifurcated or dual aspects, thereafter known as Yeshua and Mary.

---

46 *Ibid*, An updated version of the Psalm, p. 10.

The Evolution of Yeshua

Once formed and extended into physical reality, the Master Soul assumed a series of personalities during Its progressive and millennia long evolution. Let's look first at the development of the immanent form of divinity that evolved to become the male aspect of the Master Soul, namely Yeshua.

Note the sequence recorded in the Hebrew Bible. Amilius eventually became Adam, who by his partner and spiritual twin, Eve, had three sons: Abel, who was killed by his brother Cain, and then Seth who was reportedly beloved by The Lord for sponsoring settlements throughout the land.

It was through Seth's son, Enoch, however, that the young and incipient Master Soul began to blossom and advance - becoming the model Soul, greatly loved by all and capable of controlling the selfish urges that had earlier befallen the likes of Cain and such angelic figures as Lucifer. True to His divine calling, Enoch was taken body and Soul into Heaven.

According to Glenn Sanderfur (see footnote 48, below), Edgar Cayce interpreted the departure of Enoch as follow: "the people forgot what He had said and ceased to follow the ways of love and service. Even the mysteries that He had revealed were lost or were considered to be mere myths."

So the evolving Amilius/Enoch/Yeshua figure tried again, this time as Melchizedek, priest and king of the city of Jerusalem, the one who blessed Abraham upon his return from battle, and who later recognized him for his "standard of righteousness for proper living and love." [47] So revered was Melchizedek that He too was taken directly into Heaven upon his physical death. Unfortunately, the people then thought it impossible to follow His example - and so gradually returned to their selfish habits. [48]

Yeshua's subsequent development came with his incarnation as the famed Joseph, born to Rachel and Jacob in their old age. Young Joseph was

---

47 Gen. 14: 17-20; and Ps.110:4; Heb. 5:6,10; 6:20-7:22.
48 *Sanderfur*, op. cit., p. 17.

subsequently hated by his half-brothers, perhaps because they thought he gained too much attention as the very late newcomer to the family. Again the emerging essence of Yeshua shined through when Joseph overcame many difficulties and became the trusted and powerful assistant to the Egyptian pharaoh. Joseph then not only forgave his brothers and invited them to live with him in Egypt. He even worked to save the Egyptian people from a severe drought.

Joseph's loving development and service so advanced the unfolding of the Master Soul that It decided to incarnate again - becoming Joshua, the army commander who led the Jews into the 'Promised Land'; then Asaph, prophet, writer of some of the Psalms of the Old Testament and famed musician in the Houses of David and Solomon; and then as the priest Jeshua (still developing as 'Yeshua') who helped the Jewish people rebuild the Temple in Jerusalem upon their return from captivity in Babylon.

Continuing Development

The masculine side of the Master Soul continued to incarnate far and wide, beyond the borders of Palestine and the issues faced by the Jewish people. He also incarnated, for example, as Zend of Persia whose son, Zoroaster had propagated the belief in a single and benevolent deity, the eventual triumph of good over evil, the presence of a heaven and a hell, and the conclusion that everyone possessed a free will. These spiritual notions dominated the philosophy of the Middle East for much of the millennia spanning 600 BCE to 650 CE.

Thus has the masculine side of the Master Soul continued to appear throughout history as such cultural figures as Hermes of Egypt, Rama of Egypt, Confucius of China, and Buddha in India and Japan. [49] Yeshua also appeared as the revered spirit of Japanese Taoism, and as a leader of a host of North American Indian tribes, including the Hopi and Navajo of

---

49 Sanderfur, *op cit,* p. 36.

Arizona, the Shoshone of Nevada, the Chippewa of Montana, the Oglala-Lakota tribe of Wyoming, the Wampanoag of Massachusetts and the Ojibwa of the Great Lakes area. [50]

Of late, Yeshua has reportedly chosen to alternate His appearances between such varied figures as a beggar, young professor, bartender, librarian, clerk, manager, steel worker and ordinary resident of various areas of the world. [51] Yeshua always appears in disguise, assuming the stance and dress of the local area He visits. He reportedly works His wonders through the simple radiation of His presence, giving advice when asked, curing people as He naturally greets and passes among them. He reportedly stays in a particular setting for as long as He is needed but will return to it if called - always flexible, always ready yet always willing to move on wherever He senses He is needed next.

The Female Energy

The historic figure we know as the biblical Mother Mary became the female aspect of the Master Soul when She gave birth to Yeshua and had Her divine status confirmed by Her subsequent Assumption into Heaven.

Like Her male counterpart, Mother Mary slowly established Her role as a Master Soul, appearing throughout the ages under many different

---

50 Confirmed by Gabriel (Benu) in direct conversations, 2019-22.

51 According to Benu, Yeshua continues to vary His physical appearances according to perceived need and interest - periodically rotating His exact locations in order to assist as many different groups and areas as possible - often doing so simultaneously(!). His frequent appearances among the Native American tribes have included becoming such leaders as Black Elk of the Oglala-Lakota Sioux, Massacoit of the Wampanoug, and Crazy Horse of the Lakota people.

Also See William Francis Sturner, *Yeshua: The Continuing Presence of the Master Soul* (Osprey, FL: CreateSpace, 2017).

guises. According to the Hebrew-Christian Bible, She appears initially as Sophia, the prehistoric Eve, Mother of Life itself. She then appeared as Sarah, who at ninety years old conceived Isaac, died eventually at the age of 127 and was heralded as a symbol of faith and trust in the Divine; Miriam, considered a prophet, kept watch over Moses after he was hidden in the reeds by his Jewish mother following the Pharaoh's order to slay all Jewish newborn boys, and who then led the women in hymns of prayer after crossing the Red Sea; and Rebekah, who conspired to have Jacob blessed by Isaac as the first-born thus passing over his twin, Esau.[52]

Mary's many other biblical appearances subsequently included Deborah, the grandmother who raised the orphan, Tobit, and taught him to follow the Laws of Moses; Esther, who at the time of Xerxes and Mordecai, foiled a plot to destroy the Jews; and Hagar, the maid of Sarah who conceived the son of Abraham, named him Ishmael - who was later honored as a prophet of Islam.

Her development as the female aspect of the Master Soul was then completed with Her incarnation as the Mother of Yeshua and Her subsequent Assumption into Heaven. [53] Mary has since appeared frequently during the modern era. Dressed in biblical attire She has spoken directly with children and adults in such diverse areas as Fatima, Portugal; Rome, Italy; Aika, Japan; Lourdes, France; and Mexico City, Mexico.

And like Yeshua, She too has appeared as a variety of personalities in a host of settings: a child, maiden, wood-worker, physician, store owner, passerby - you name it - staying for only a moment or two; or in residence for days or weeks as determined by Her particular mission.

---

52 M.L del Mastro, *Woman of the Bible* (Edison, NJ: Castle Books, 2004); and Patricia Monaghan, *Divinedesses and Heroines* (New York: E.P. Dutton, 1981).
53 Shortly after Her Assumption, Mother Mary asked God to return Her to the Earth and the physical realm so She could continue Her work of healing. See Sturner, *The Return*, op. cit., 2022.

According to other world-wide traditions, Mother Mary's earlier incarnations have also included such diverse cultural embodiments as Kuan Yin, the bodhisattva of Mercy and Compassion; Nut, who as the Great Weaver in Egyptian mythology created the Sun and the Earth, arching her body over the material world then known as Geb; and Sophia, whom the Gnostics celebrated as the highest ruler of the visible universe, shaper of our mundane universe and in essence as the Mother of Life Itself.

Mother Mary later manifest as Aphrodite, the Olympian Goddess of love, beauty, pleasure and procreation, who was often depicted as a beautiful woman accompanied by the winged Divine Eros (Love or the Roman Cupid); Astarte, deified in Bronze Age Syrian cities as the morning and/or evening star, the counterpart of the Assyro-Babylonian divinity, Usher, the 'lady of love'; and Demeter, the Greek divinity whose daughter, Persephone was the goddess of fertility. Both also played central roles in the Eleusinian Mysteries, a religious tradition that predated the Olympian pantheon - during which the figure of Persephone in essence appeared as the Maiden (or Kore), and Demeter appeared as Mother or aged and wise Crone.

Then there was Isis, daughter of Nut and Geb, who in rejoining Osiris's dismembered body gives him eternal life, becomes the Queen of Egypt, revives the flow of the Nile and gives birth to Horus as the reborn Osiris; Athena, the ancient Greek divinity associated with wisdom, handicraft, and warfare; Penelope, the wise and enduring wife of the mythic Odysseus who remained faithful to him throughout his twenty years of explorations; and Maya, the divinity of the Earth and the Mother of all living things in the Buddhist tradition. [54]

---

54 See Joseph Campbell, *Goddesses* (New York: New World Library, 2013); Marija Gimbutas, *The Living Goddesses* (Berkeley, CA: University of California Press, 2001); David Leeming & Jake Page, *Myths of the Female Divine* (New York: Oxford University Press, 1964); and Wikipedia under the names of the various goddesses.

Love

Love is the energy of Prime Source, which when manifest reveals ITSelf as Yeshua and Mary. Love is also the universal substance that creates the physical elements and contours of the universe.

The Sacred Trio is best depicted as an equilateral triangle, with each point representing an aspect of our trio: God at the top or pinnacle, the point to the lower left as Incarnate and the point to the lower right as the Soul. The triangle is perfectly aligned within a circle, and in its center is the word *Love*. Such a figure represents the creative vigor of the cosmos - with love as its cause and its outcome.

Such is the power of 'begetting' - the term used in the Hebrew Bible to describe the capacity of human beings to also create successive waves of newborns. As human creativity has the power to create children of the mind and body, so does spiritual creativity - when consummated with unconditional love - have the power to transform everyday occurrences into the sacred happenings.

Each unfolding supports its endless capacity to generate the next, and the next manifestation of creative love. As two sides of the same coin, the forever transcendent and the everyday immanent signify the unified mission of the outer and the inner, the heavenly and the mundane, the divine and the incessant service of soulful incarnates.

Such is the desired connection between the proverbial you and I. It is the energy that is missing when strife and rancor rule the day. It is the child, the sacred building, the poem, the friendship, and the physical being generated in the fusion of mutual love. Ultimately, it is the eternal coupling of creative energies generating ever-more-effective forms, the urge to transcendence when carried into the presence of the everyday, God's eternal love being manifest in and through your actions and mine.

Chapter Four. The Blessed Alignment

Unified, Ubiquitous, Perpetual

Spiritual Truths

THE TRUTHS OF SPIRITUAL LIFE EMERGE EVER SO CLEARLY WHEN viewed from the perspective of what is *'supposedly true'* in comparison to what has been established as *'reality'*.

1. Supposedly True: Life is exactly as it appears on the surface: we are born, live, adjust, slow down and die.

Reality: We each and all exist in a much larger context - for we are immortal Souls, now incarnated on Earth as people who play varied roles as we try to complete various spiritual missions. Initially and ultimately, We embodied Souls are empowered to make a spiritual difference as we strengthen our ability to act with love and compassion.

2. Supposedly: As soulful incarnates the best we can do spiritually is belong to an established religion, abide by its edicts and obey its authorities.

Reality: We have all sorts of options to serve spiritually – inside a religion if we wish, perhaps allying with one religion or spiritual group or another, or by acting on one's own to honor God directly, praying and mediating as we wish, freed from the catechisms, timetables and edicts of intermediaries.

3. Supposedly: You and I each have an immortal Soul.

Realty: Each of us IS an immortal Soul.

4. Supposedly: We are nothing but an immortal Soul.

Reality: Everyone - including the person reading these lines - is the bodily incarnation of an immortal Soul. We humans are a unification of both sides of the same coin: an immortal Soul who has become an incarnate in order to instill the love of Heaven in the physical realm.

5. Supposedly: As human incarnates we are separated from the intentions and empowerment of our Souls.

Reality: We are composites of body, mind and Soul – as indicated in the identities of our three aspects of the Sacred Trio: Body, Soul and Divine - or Me, My Self and Spirit. There is no separation, only interpenetration and mutual interdependence.

6. Supposedly: In my current existence, I am immortal.

Reality: The incarnated aspects of my identity – my body and mind (including my emotions) – are subject to the laws of the physical world and thus to deterioration and death. The formative aspect of our identity – namely our respective Souls - are immortal and have been empowered throughout history to create a series of embodiments.

7. Supposedly: As immoral Souls, we are able to incarnate or commission a new embodiment and thus enter into the physical domain any time we wish.

Reality: Once a current embodiment has passed, We may, with The Lord's consent and encouragement, continue to invoke the process of incarnation and both create and become a series of successive embodiments in the physical realm.

8. Supposedly: When we incarnate, we must as Souls leave our Heavenly abode completely in order to embed ourselves in our new incarnate.

Reality: As Souls we only need to infuse a relatively small portion (usually ten percent) of our prodigious soul-energy into our new incarnate in order to guide (but not dictate) its intentions and actions.

9. Supposedly: Once born and embedded into an incarnate in the material domain, we Soul-incarnates are left to fend for ourselves.

Reality: As immortal Souls we are and remain integral components of God and thus maintain direct access to and contact with Prime Source, including such varied aspects of the spiritual world as Archangels, Angels, Ascended Masters and other sacred energies that assist in the governance of the cosmos (such as the Seraphim, Cherubim, etc.). [55]

10. Supposedly: Once born into the material realm, the incarnate is free to exercise ITs own judgment.

Reality: The Soul-incarnate is always free to exercise its free will and make Its own decisions – although it is counseled to act with love and compassion given It's Soul's direct connection to Prime Source as one of ITs cosmic cells or components.

11. Supposedly: An incarnate is on ITs own once it enters the physical domain.

Reality: The full Soul that resides in Heaven continues to guide the portion of Itself that is embedded as an incarnate. Therefore, the Soul is able to guide but not necessarily direct the incarnate as it faces the challenges and temptations of the created realm.

12. Supposedly: The portion of the Soul embedded in the incarnate evaporates upon the death of the entity that housed it.

Reality: Upon the demise of an embodiment, the part of the Soul that was embedded in it is reunited with the full Soul in the heavenly domain.

13: Supposedly: The death of an embodiment ends a Soul's involvement in the incarnational process.

Reality: Following the demise of a given embodiment, the Soul enters into an intensive review of the life It just led in unison with Its incarnate. Then, It will either reconnect directly with Its Core group of soulful friends and associates, obtain whatever additional training and schooling is deemed

---

55 See below, 'What Then of Prime Source'.

necessary, and based on The Lord's timing, anticipate being asked to form a new incarnate.

As approved by God, the Soul may at some juncture re-enter the material sphere as a new incarnate, adopt a new name and mission and embed Itself in the newborn, as usual, just as the newborn is delivered into the world of everyday living.

14. Supposedly: Upon Its death, the memory and contributions of a given incarnate are forgotten and discarded.

Reality: The history of the life and learnings of each incarnate is recorded for all eternity in the Akashic Record, the cumulative memory of which is available to each successive incarnate. Such cumulative memories were stored - for consultation and guidance - at the base of the skull of each new embodiment.

Therefore

As immortal Souls in human clothing, we really are from another world, our bodies and minds having been created in order to give us the means of fulfilling our earthly mission - to think and act with love and compassion and thereby help fulfill the spiritual enlightenment of the physical universe.

As embodied Souls, formed by and as components of the heavenly domain, We are in essence extra-terrestrials.

As extra-terrestrials, we appear on Earth bearing a blend of the facial and bodily characteristics of our incarnate's human parents, and thereafter work on implementing the intentions outlined in the life scripts We had chosen earlier with the consent of our budding embodiments.

Analogs of the Sacred Trinity

There are all sorts of analogs to the relationships ascribed to the Sacred Trio as body, spirit and divine. Most are drawn from everyday life. Others invoke the terminology of religion, philosophy, astronomy and the sciences. None of them necessarily fit the circumstances of the others, but each set of analogies adds insight into how the connections between My Body, My Soul and My Divine Lord operate. Here is a sample.

Perceptually the sequence of such a trio could be described as 'insight, inspiration and vision'. In terms of everyday living the best descriptors might be 'mundane, other worldly and enlightened' or 'immediate, intermediate and long-range'. The descriptions of 'example, category and genus' also capture the relationships well as do 'instance, pattern and model'. Then there is 'moral, immortal and eternal'.

Biologically the threesome would be rendered as 'cell, molecule and organ' and philosophically as 'notion, idea and truth'. In a colloquial sense it might be best to say 'novice, journeyman and adept' or 'student, teacher, and dean'. And how could we forget the progression of 'smiling, joyful and exuberant', 'stargazer, astronaut and cosmonaut' or 'Earth, Milky Way and Universe'. In terms of process, the relationships might invoke 'a hike, a tour and an adventure' or be described as 'limited, enhanced and perfect'.

'Player, coach and manager' would cover the athletic side, 'id, ego and superego' would please the Freudians and 'Larry, Curly and Moe' would surely capture the essence of the trio for those who love vaudeville and Hollywood.

Energy Flows

Now, let's retrace the energy flow between the three aspects of the Sacred Trinity from various perspectives. Thus far our review has proceeded progressively from the earthly human, to the intermediary or immortal Soul, to the Creator or Prime Source ITSelf. Let's continue that sequence.

An analogous unfolding of life can be traced from the most common to the higher reaches of consciousness: humanoids were evident around three million years ago, sentient homo sapiens appearing some 150 thousand years thereafter, with our 'modern' strand of self-conscious humans surfacing approximately 40,000 years ago.

We could also reverse fields and look at the Sacred Trio as beginning with God the creative instigator of it All, then at how IT dissolved into soulful or intermediary forms, which in turn were infused into our immediate physical figures or incarnates.

Similarly, look as the analogs displayed in the formation of the physical universe. The Big Bang, like Prime Source, has been the causal agent for the emergence and development of the physical universe. And just as we modern humans are thus physically rooted in the chemical abundance unleashed with the Big Bang, so have our psycho-spiritual capacities in turn brought about a series of creative developments that are grounded in the earth.

Look at the natural development of the human species, which when traced along Darwinian lines shows the most adaptable of life's forms progressively advancing - eventually narrowing to the humanoid and homo sentient-sentient human species.

Other advances stemmed from the prevalence of wormholes and their capacity to facilitate the flow and translocation of extraterrestrial Souls who thus were able to travel from their various galactic and planetary systems and assist in the continuous the development our planet Earth.

Thus Life on Earth grew in sophistication with the influx of wave after wave of extraterrestrial forces, their DNA greatly enhancing the powers of the local species, and resulted in the building of what can only be considered the greatest set of wonders ever created throughout the various parts of our Earth. The building of the many incredible structures noted below, with their many intricate engineering marvels and intricacies simply could not have happened without the input of a successive wave of extraterrestrials who possessed superior knowledge.

Consider, for example, Göbekli Tepe, known as the world's oldest temple, built approximately 12,000 years ago in south-east Turkey in the pre-pottery Neolithic period before writing or the wheel, and thus many millennia before the emergence of the famed Stonehenge or Egypt's great pyramids.

The wonders thus also include the enormous stone columns of Stonehenge and the thousands of huge blocks of stone that constitute Egypt's great pyramids, the seven million year old temples on Malta, the

Moai sculptures on Easter Island, and the gigantic drawings in the stone cliffs at Nazca, Peru.

Then there are the enormous blocks of jointed stone still in place at such cites as Sacsahuaman near Cusco, Peru; the many juggernaut temples and palaces of Teotihuacan (north of the current Mexico City); the wondrously intricate Crop Circles which for years were mysteriously carved into the wheat fields of southern England; and the incredibly precise astrological alignments that are integral to the numerous structures built into the many structures of Machu Pincchu in Peru. And on and on and on.

No mere set of human hands had created such achievements. Waves of extra-terrestrials - with their obviously superior knowledge and know-how - surely worked with each generation of enhanced residents to achieve the series of miraculous and heavenly structures outlined here. [56]

Which Came First

Theorists and theologians have considered such issues since time immemorial – reaching many varied conclusions and espousing different explanations of two major issues. One is the relationship between the expression of ITS outer or physical universe, and ITS inner or spiritual

---

[56] The sources of information are numerous and detailed. Consult, for example, references to the structures mentioned as listed on the internet, and to Amazon in particular. Also see the references made on any general encyclopedia including Wikipedia.

In particular, view any and all of the 135 episodes of *Ancient Aliens,* presented for ten seasons on PBS television and now available on DVD.

As to specific books, read the many testimonies of Dolores Cannon including *The Convoluted Universe;* Erich von Daniken's *Chariots of the Gods*; and the findings of psychologist, Michael Newton who in *Journey of Souls*, and *Destiny of Souls* was able to elicit and record the profound spiritual experiences of his patient/clients.

evolution. The other is the relationship between the other-worldly and transcendent nature of Prime Source, and ITS appearance in the physical world as the immanent presence of the Master Soul.

In both forms - the outer or physical, the inner or spiritual, and the transcendent and immanent - Prime Source is revealed at IT's core to be ever changing, ever developing, always reaching for higher and deeper modes of Being. Through it all, IT displays ITs powers to be virtuous, loving, omnipotent (all powerful) and omniscient (all knowing). IT also appears as ubiquitous - evident everywhere in and as both eternally cosmic and present everywhere in the everyday.

Likewise, IT created the unity of the cosmos in the name of love and in so doing expressed that same compassion in ITs unfolding within the physical realm. IT is both above and below, beyond the comprehension of our three-dimensional minds yet evident to us as a series of immediate and knowable forms.

These traits set the parameters within which we can decipher and surmise the Divine's intention to enable ITs component Souls to utilize the process of incarnation to develop and then infuse themselves into generations of human incarnates. This top-down way of looking at the Sacred Trio moves progressively from the all-inclusive and causal entity of God - to Its intermediary Souls, who in turn infused themselves into the mortals, thus allowing Its heavenly gifts to be expressed in everyday reality.

Prime Source

Prime means prime – first, foremost, the only, the originating element. In mathematical terms prime is the number that has no factor but itself and one. Prime Source thus precedes all others in time, space and degree.

Source, of course, infers root, origin, beginning and the primal cause, literally defined by the *Visual Thesaurus* as 'the place where something begins or springs into being'. The source of our physical universe can be traced back to its origination in the Big Bang. As to ITs spiritual essence, the transcendent Spirit has had no beginning and has no end. IT is literally and operationally immortal and eternal.

In both Its external and internal operations, Prime Source operates through ITs Heavenly Hierarchy consisting of nine celestial orders. The orders noted here are approximations - given the human tendency to put things into categories. In reality the various aspects of the Divine may lie closer to emphases in function with a great deal interpenetration and the sharing of tasks.

And so we refer to the Seraphrim, beings of pure light, reportedly in direct contact with God, and who resonate to the Fire of Love; the Cherubrim, known for their wisdom and knowledge, bearers later of the Ark of the Covenant and guardians to the Tree of Life, each one - as later depicted physically, having four faces and four wings (as subsequently witnessed by the prophet Ezekiel: 1:4-28); and the Thrones, also later depicted as great wheels containing many eyes and residing at the edge of the transcendent cosmos where the physical universe begins to unfold.

Then there are the Dominations, the channels of mercy who also supervise the duties of the angels; the Virtues who escorted Yeshua to Heaven during His Ascension and which bestow God's grace in the form of miracles; and the Powers which patrol the borders of heaven and help the immortal Souls or cells of Prime Source overcome any egotistic tendencies they may experience as incarnates. [57]

A third triad consists of the Principalities, Archangels and Angels. The Principalities are the channels of mercy, and guardians of civilizations especially their cultures and cities. Once the guardians of religion, they are aides to Yeshua and Mary now that they have developed into the fulness of their twin aspects of the Master Soul.

---

57 Rosemary Ellen Guiley, *The Encyclopedia of Angels* (New York: Checkmark Books: Facts on File, 2004).

The four Archangels who appear most frequently in spiritual lore are Michael, usually depicted with a sword, the undisputed hero and opposing force of any who allege to be or sponsor the lore of Satan, who later stayed the hand of Abraham when he was about to slay Isaac, and who appeared to Moses at the time of the burning bush.

Then there is Gabriel, the governor of Eden, the famous Archangel of Mercy, the divine messenger of conceptions including of course the Annunciation of Mary, and who represents the aspect of Heaven which by word and action is the closest to humankind. Gabriel's closest associate is Raphael, 'the shining one who heals', depicted in the Bible teaching Tobit how to use parts of the fish he caught to heal others. Raphael is also known for his joyful and childlike love of interacting with and guiding others.

Completing the Heavenly Hierarchy are the slew of angels and the many messengers of the Lord - couriers and intermediaries who carry out the more immediate and specific phases of heavenly guidance. They often work very closely with one of the Archangels in particular, such as Sarah, Jason and Zachary help to carry out the intentions of our beloved Gabriel.

In short, the many aspects of the Heavenly Hierarchy play a role in safe-guarding, supervising and carrying out Prime Source's cosmic, multi-dimensional and immediate tasks and activities - thus enabling The Divine to leave Its imprint on everyone and everything. [58]

External Expansion

How Prime Source operates can be deduced in part by examining the operations of the universe IT created. As noted, the eternal and

---

[58] See Pseudo-Dionysius the Areopogite (Greek author of the 5th-6 Century), *Celestial Hierarchy (Surrey, England: Garden City Press Ltd., 1935)*; Thomas Aquinas's *Summa Theologiae: A Guide and Commentary* by Brian Davies (New York, Oxford University, 2014: see in particular references to *1.108 and 6.7)*.

transcendental God simply exists forever, has no beginning and has no end. As the creative energy of the universe, however, IT can call forth ITs component cells and activate ITs continuous expansion - as is evident in the Big Bang and subsequent observations of our astronomers. ITs expansive intentions produced the chemical elements (as listed in the periodic scale), then the atomic structures and chemical combinations of the physical cells and molecules that became the building blocks for the formation of the ensuing billions of galaxies, stars and planetary systems that comprise our physical universe.

Depth and Internal Soulfulness

It addition to ITS external expansion, Prime Source also attained truly prodigious internal or spiritual depth when IT created the billions of Souls that comprise ITs reality. In other words, Prime Source eventually used Us - as immortal cells or parts of ITSelf - to create ITs representatives in the everyday world of the earthy reality. By instituting the process of incarnation, Prime Source enabled You and Me - ITS component Souls - to form physical embodiments of Ourselves by infusing a hefty portion of Our soulfulness into an increasingly progressive set of incarnates. Thus, did We - repositories of a divine heritage - become the very people who demonstrate divinity's daily presence in our everyday universe.

Adding to this phenomenal transformation, consider the direct entry of God Itself into Our world of everyday materiality through the incarnation of Yeshua and Mary as the male and female aspects the Master Soul.

As noted in the analogies listed earlier, as incarnations of Our immortal Souls we are the crucial links between divine purpose and ITs realization in the material world. 'Tinkers-to-Evans-to-Chance' was the parlance of baseball for many years that depicted the seamless unity of the double-play combo of the former Chicago Cubs - an apt analog for the Divine Trio of *Incarnate-to-Soul-to-Divinity* - or its kissing cousins: God - to ITs Souls - to Their incarnates in the world of everyday living. *Automatic, self-activating,* and with *immediate through-put:* the modern terms for describing how the creator of Life, sends ITs agents of compassion, into our world to sponsor and sustain the essence of love.

Focus on the Soul

Yet even the flow between the three parts of the trio needs to be sparked by willful intent, and that immediately links us back to the role of the Soul. As an integral part of The Divine, each Soul (like you and I) plays an essential role in activating the process of incarnation. Like the physical progression of a cell, to a molecule as the many varied aspects and organs of the physical body emerge, we Souls play an essential role in the creation, recreation and continual unfolding of The Lord.

We Souls - by supplementing our immortal status with a mortal incarnate embodiment - exemplify the process used by the transcendent Divine to attain a similar end, that is to invoke the immanent presence of the Master Soul (Yeshua/Mary). And we do so - automatically every hour of everyday - by simply acting through our daily experiences as citizens of this glorious region known as Earth.

As immortal Souls we must ask The Lord to embody ourselves in the physical realm. Once approved, We infuse a portion of Ourselves into Our mortal embodiments, thereby fulfilling our soulful intention to instill love and compassion into this created environment.

Of course, as would-be incarnates, we thereby agree to do everything we can to complete the pledges we made prior to incarnation. And off we went - attracting the desired and intended physical parents, assisting the emergent fetus as it matures over nine months, waiting at the mouth of the uterus, completing a 'double-check' and then placing a sufficient amount of Our soulfulness behind heart of the emerging child just as the newborn emerges into the outer world at the moment of its physical birth. [59]

---

59 This may help to diffuse the debate between the advocates of pro-life and pro-choice. The abortion of a fetus means its growth is terminated prior to

Loving and Empowered Incarnate

Now for the third element in the Sacred Trip - the lowest in the hierarchy but the one we know best for it constitutes the essence our daily life.

Note how the parents - and especially the Mother of every species is imbued with a similar protective and caring instinct: to guard and feed the newborn, love it and nurture it until it can care for itself. Such characteristics are especially well honed by We sentient-sentient beings (self-aware or *aware of our awareness*). You and I thus pass through the threshold and become the esteemed objects of our spiritual inquiry.

While young, the newborn is still aware of the fact that It continues to be an immortal. Yet as a newborn it also senses it has carried the gift of living into everyday reality.

In short, as an abiding Soul the newborn knowingly continues to experience its divine heritage and blessed with an amazing bundle of empowerments. The new being thereby naturally yearns to exercise Its capacity to can grow and develop – and initially that means exponentially.

Thus do Our movements, skills and dexterities expand rapidly. We eat, cry, sleep, begin to crawl and suddenly one day we trust ourselves to stand, walk and then run just about everywhere - the newness of it all motivating Us to explore and be one with everything within reach.

Spiritually, We - as newborn incarnates - experience Our new world as a stranger in a strange land. As embedded Souls We remember the heavenly domain for several months after Our incarnate birth and continue to

---

being 'delivered' or born. An abortion, however, does not amount to the killing of a child.

It is crucial to remember that the Soul is not infused into the newborn until the exact moment of its birth or delivery. Therefore an abortion only stops the growth of a fetus and does not amount to the termination of a fully constituted soulful child or person.

cherish Our linkage to the cosmic body of Prime Source. Yet We begin to realize We are also serving in an additional role: the incarnate of an immortal cell of The Lord has also become a soulful human being playing a distinct and purposeful role in a new and increasingly strange land.

So how is this new entity, this new combination of body, mind and spirit, this unique blend of immortal Soul and mortal ego expected to operate if it is to honor both sides of its identity? Its pre-natal training as a Soul enables It to choose the 'right' thing and be a true and steady presentative of God on earth. Yet simultaneous human status enables It to exercise our free will as we learn to live and prosper in a world of many options.

That means the likes of you and I - and all the other Souls who have ever chosen to incarnate - will often experience the dilemma of pitting our divinely appointed role against the demands of the earthly environment we were commissioned to transform. We realize more fully each day, especially with each passing stage of maturity, that We incarnate Souls have also assumed an enormous set of responsibilities in a world whose physical and mental-emotional constructs mirror the priorities - not of Our heavenly home but our new physical world. What a wondrous being We are and yet still asked to become: a soulful person born of the heavens yet living in the world of everyday expectations and challenges.

Who Have You Been?

It is highly unusual for a given Soul to incarnate only once. The millennia of human history are filled with Our predecessors, spiritual ancestors and contributing extensions - all the earlier embodied expressions of Our respective Souls.

Memories of Our Soul's earlier lifetimes are filed in the memory bank stored at the base of the scull of every new incarnate, and are available for consultation any time any of our subsequent embodiments invoke our essence and advice. We each carry within us the complete history of Our Souls' earlier appearances – complete with all of Their previous intentions, promises, actions, miscues, setbacks and contributions.

Access to this warehouse of information is now available to you upon request. In response, the desired information could appear to you as images in your sleep, as messages that suddenly or repeatedly appear in print, or as overwhelming feelings and repeated insights that emerge as you walk, talk, pray or meditate.

Upon the death of an embodiment, the total record of images accumulated during a lifetime - contributions, warts, and all - is transferred by your Soul to its cumulative memory bank, where it is automatically transferred to the base of the skull of the next or newest incarnate.

Patterns and Themes

We have already outlined My Soul's list of earlier embodiments and thus the antecedents to My incarnation as William. Let us now add some significant details and fill in the profile – allowing us to more thoroughly trace the history of incarnations formed by My immortal Soul Aeneas. In particular, let's see if any of the themes developed by William have also been pursued by any of My earlier incarnates.

As we proceed, you - the reader - might allow yourself to recall the names and experiences of your Soul's former spiritual-physical embodiments – going back as far as your mediations and consultations with your stored images take you. Perhaps such recalls will enable you to identify the history of some of your current needs, interests and skills as continuations or carryovers from previous lifetimes. Be sensitive as well to any new themes or pronounced changes in the range and intensity of earlier ones.

It may be difficult to trace a direct line between the past and the present, between the abilities, attitudes and interests of your Soul's previous incarnations and those you display today. But it is worth the try; there are insights to be uncovered. As the boy is the father to the man (who said that: Wordsworth?), whatever has transpired can yield fascinating insights into where you are heading now.

Let's take My current experiences as William as an example. Four major themes have emerged, beginning with his relatively prescribed notion of religion - subsequently experienced as a more inclusive affirmation of spirituality.

Religious Turned Spiritual

My current incarnate William's earliest, continuous and most dominant memories have revolved around his belief and avid participation in the structured religion of Catholicism. As outlined in one of My earlier books as William, he was a dedicated church goer throughout his early life, the one who was designated by his family to say grace at meals and on whom the it could depend to express a so-called religious point of view. [60]

By his early twenties he was a daily communicant – getting up at 5:00 every morning to walk to the local church before grabbing a buttered roll or Danish and then catching a bus or train to school or work. Daily Mass at the near-by Italian geographic Catholic church invariably attracted only a few elderly ladies, a middle-aged workman or two and William – each sitting rows apart, never interacting, meeting only briefly at the altar-rail with folded hands and open-mouths.

The older he got, the wider his interactions grew - and with them came a new set of questions, doubts, and an expanded sense of life's moral complexity. A set of experiences involving what he considered cleric hypocrisy was greatly intensified one evening when he was condemned by the clerical leader and many of his fellow for disagreeing with what he considered the unconstitutional edicts of the local bishop.

Diminished devotion then followed in memorable intervals: he stopped going to confession, then Mass - and soon was no longer on the defensive but was overtly looking for any defect he could find in the Church's official viewpoint. Within months William became a reverse crusader - now storming the very vulnerable walls of what he once considered a revered and impregnable castle. As it turned out, he did not have to

---

60 *Trust Your Immortal Soul, op. cit.,* in particular, Chapter 5.

look very far to find a reason to protest and then outwardly reject any - and then all - of the official ways of the Church.

What strikes Me now is that this theme of rebellion was also highlighted in the lives of many of My previous incarnations. As noted above, I, Aeneas - had incarnated earlier as a priest to Akhenaten, the pharaoh who caused an enormous upheaval in Egyptian society when he denounced its long adherence to polytheism and chose instead to worship the divine that he called Aten.

Other examples include being a student of such dissenting prophets as Judaism's Amos, Ezekiel and Elijah; to incarnating later as the infamous Origen (183-263 ACE), the early Church 'Father' and prolific theologian whose condemnation of the doctrine of original sin stirred up so much trouble that he - Origen - was finally excommunicated from the Catholic Church a few centuries later.

I also embodied as Marcion of Sinope, who condemned what he considered the many of malevolent gods revered in the Old Testament, maintaining - throughout his career - that Yeshua, not the Jewish Yahweh - was the true expression of God. As Clement of Alexandria, I, Aeneas, was also condemned by early church officials for espousing the works of Plato and the Stoics.

During the 3rd century of Egypt, one of My predecessors was an avid student of Hermes Trismegistus, the legendary combination of the Greek god Hermes and the Egyptian god Thoth. I also played a dissenting role as Pelagius (354-418), the Neo-Platonist British monk who emphasized the right of all Souls to choose salvation, and who was highly critical of the degrading behavior of the Christians of Rome. Then came Plotinus of Egypt (204-270), who argued for a complex cosmology based on an interpretation of Plato known as Neoplatonism, and Libanius (314-392), who remained a staunch defender of Greek paganism despite the emerging dominance of the Catholic Church.

Subsequently one of My earlier incarnations was as Fra Teofilo de Vairano, an advisor to Giordano Bruno (1548-1660), the Dominion friar, mathematician and astronomer who was condemned by the Church in 1600 for supporting Copernicus' discovery that our universe was infinite in expanse, and that it not only had no particular center but consisted of many planets, each of which could sustain a form of life.

Writing and Communication

The historical record also demonstrates that I - Aeneas - had incarnated throughout history as a series of people who loved to write. Witness the continuities between John the Apostle, author of the Fourth Gospel of the Bible and several epistles; the incredibly prolific, Origen, the theologian of the 3rd Century who authored no less than 2,000 treaties on all phases of theology; Thomas Traherne, a poet and writer of the 16th century; and more contemporaneously, Charles Williams of Inkling fame who wrote several very popular books on spiritual-mythic themes.

I also incarnated as colleagues and close friends of such famed writers as Thoreau and Emerson and the poet Walt Whitman, each of whom espoused transcendentalism, an approach that emphasized intuitive insights into their spiritual experiences versus the highly empiric and rational approaches favored by the prevalent denominations.

My desire to express Myself in writing has also been evident throughout this current incarnation. Several of William's articles and poems were published in his grammar school publication newspaper. Later he became a reporter and columnist for his high school newspaper; majored in journalism in college, became an editor and weekly columnist for his college newspaper, then went on to complete a masters in communications, become a writer for the University of Wisconsin, was awarded an internship to serve as the assistant to the managing editor of *The Washington Post*, and after completing his doctorate wrote eight books on creativity and organizational change, adding seven more titles later on the various themes of spirituality.

Questioning Authority

Many of My series of incarnates have also had a tendency to question authority. None of them apparently played leading roles in the French, English or American Revolutions (although one of them apparently participated in the storming of the Bastille on July 14, the day of William's birthday). William also has displayed a marked ability to successfully challenge authority when confronted with what he perceived as an injustice. For example, he successfully petitioned the dean of his college to reverse the decision of a teacher who had drastically reduced his grade for an alleged social miscue; and later filed a formal complaint that led to the dismissal of a revered superior for incompetence.

Later he successfully appealed up the chain of command and thus forced his Army sergeant to reverse a discriminatory decision; petitioned the Governor's office to countermand an invidious decision made by the commanding officer of his Army Reserve; forced a recalcitrant local sanitation official to pick up heaps of cumulative garbage near his home by writing to the Mayor of NewYorkCity; and, as noted, challenged what he considered the unconstitutional edict of the local Cardinal which resulted in his being summarily expelled from a Catholic action group.

Healing

Then there's the issue of awakening one's power of healing - an energy that is inherent in every incarnate if only they would affirm and activate it. My current incarnate, however, slowly became aware of his capacity to serve as a very effective intermediary. Upon sensing the need in another, He would momentarily quiet himself and become a channel for the healing energies of The Lord to pass through him to the intended other. He could do so at any time he sensed a need, including while he innocently passed someone on the street, at a gathering or in a supermarket.

Again, all incarnates, all persons now living on Earth - including you, the reader - are empowered to act as an intermediary for the transmission of The Lord's healing powers. The difference is that some incarnates have simply learned to trust in their capacity to act as a channel for The Lord's healing powers - and 'step into that role' when so inspired.

The perennial question: have any of My much earlier incarnates expressed such an ability? As noted above, I as the Soul, Aeneas, incarnated earlier as Asclepius, the divine spirit of the Greek pantheon who later became the doctor of medicine and founded healing centers throughout Greece in the late 6th and early 7th centuries, BCE. I also incarnated as a priest serving the pharaoh Akhenaten; in other appearances I served as a student to a series of Judaic prophets; in many other cases, I became an apprentice to a series of spiritual leaders/healers throughout Egypt and Europe.

In Summary

Thus did the themes of spirituality, questioning authority, writing and healing wind their way through many of My incarnations. They are thus likely to appear again and again in My future incarnates since they are likely to follow in the same well-established patterns - all of which were probably approved if not chosen by The Lord ITSelf. Surely any sharp deviations from the now historical pattern seem unlikely at this juncture – with a future incarnate choosing to become a very conservative member of the College of Cardinals, a political sycophant, extreme extrovert or an established atheist - - although one never knows. If so, they might emerge as such in order to broaden My repertoire, enabling Me to empathize more fully with a host of perspectives My past list of incarnates have seemed to challenge and avoid.

Just look at the total mass of incarnates The Lord has sponsored, enabled and allowed throughout the centuries - as expressed through one Soul or another: avatars and great spiritual leaders, statesmen and stateswomen as well as rogues, criminals and dictators - and everything in-between. Perhaps IT's overall capacity to become and express such a diverse combination of cosmic personalities suggests that absolutely nothing has been ruled out of bounds for what The Lord will sponsor, tolerate or allow in the created realm.

Surely such a range of possibilities may emerge again in the future. If so, does the historical record of My - and most recently, William's established clustering, indicate a sign of depth or narrowness, diversity or shallowness, a developed repertoire or just being stuck? Does experiencing bits of the esteemed on the one hand and the devious on the other help to develop empathy for every option or just lukewarm compassion for nothing in particular?

I emphasize - once again - that some of My 20,000 incarnates have surely been nasty rogues and defamers. Surely, not all of your earlier appearances have been perfect citizens and advocates of love and joy either. Are repeats of My - and your nay-to-wells - still possible? Ah: We best step lightly and be disposed to learn and evolve with whatever type of incarnate We may be encouraged to become come next - suggesting that We best prep for our next appearance by filling Our knapsacks with a trumpet or two, some protein bars and more than a few 'humble pills'.

Yet it is possible that the major themes of My - and Your - many incarnate appearances have and will continue to help in furthering the loving and creative intentions of The Lord. At least we have a right to feel that way - given the grooves We have already helped or agreed to establish.

Either way, We - together with the billions of incarnates generated by an untold number of immortal Souls - have helped to express a fine sample of Life's infinite possibilities - within which there resides a fascinating set of god-like wannabes and loving potentialities just waiting for their chance to be born.

The Other Side of the Ledger

Obviously - and fortunately - the work and emerging capacities of My current incarnate are still in process. Some deficiencies may be evident and difficulties have occurred but seemingly none of them major. It seems, however, that in toto more than one of My earthly appearances did indeed meet My expectations and may even have added to My recordings of love and compassion.

Statistically, it would also not be surprising to find that several of My incarnations have involved decisions and lifestyles that either avoided or were unable to meet the outcomes defined during their training prior to incarnation. Missing the mark with one or more of My incarnates may have added - in some undefinable way - to their range of experiences without detracting from My Soul's capacity to overcome such mishaps in subsequent incarnations. Overall, the expectation is not to attain perfection but to make progress on whatever gaps in know-how and ability emerged earlier and still contribute to the progress of love and compassion.

Take, for instance, the stubborn appearance of *impatience*. Whatever the baggage from My earlier incarnates, William often is not able to get out of his own way - still erupting occasionally at what he considers (and actually are) very incompetent and rude drivers. Similar fits of impatience also kick in at the silliest of times: while waiting in line at the grocery, when looking for the right tool to fix something or when put on hold for more than three minutes. Even the extra time needed to find the right words to complete a sentence in a new manuscript can occasionally drive William into the kitchen needing to splash some cold water on his face.

Magnifying a molehill into a mountain is no fun – and then facing the fact that you are doing it all over again can be very exasperating. Sometimes William finds it difficult to let go of a perceived slight, but at least he has now learned to regain composure within minutes - whereas in the past he may have taken a perceived grievance to bed with him. He has learned, however, to literally neutralize his anger and impatience by treating them as thorns that needed to be brushed off his clothing - and thus his psyche.

Aha: Back to the Positive

On the other hand, William is most indebted to whoever in the list of his predecessors passed on their capacity to muster a daily sense of 'mission' and a positive view of the future. He also loves his ingrained sense of aloneness and capacity to thrive as a tribe of one - yet is also in the process of learning how to overcome occasional bouts of loneliness.

A friend once described him as "a very sociable loner". That indeed is indeed him to a tee: He loves interacting with others, loves to laugh and play, greatly enjoys dancing, sharing comments and old stories, and does indeed miss many of the lovely women who have graced his life.

BUT – there is a clear limit to William's social interactions: it does not take much time for him to yearn to retreat, to again covet his alone time, process his thoughts and experiences, ponder the fate of the world and invoke the spiritual forces that surround us. Reading and writing and learning are high on his list of delights - unencumbered by any person or errand, delighted by the capacity to breathe free, mediate and just allow himself to connect with whatever his inners call forth.

Interacting with other introverts who are also willing - occasionally - to venture out into the land of hustle and bustle - helps add zest and energy to his life, but to no one's surprise - he finds that such flexible introverts are hard to find. In the interim he finds it both entertaining - and at times confusing - to watch and vicariously enjoy the antics of the ingrained extroverts. But if you love - above all - to research and gather, meditate and write, compose e-mails no less a book – then you also have reason to give thanks for your current incarnate's ability to discover and celebrate the simple yet wondrous things of Life.

We Are One

The mantra of *Me, My Immortal Soul and the Manifest Divine* merely point to the three aspects of constant unfolding of Body-Soul-Spirit but which in reality really are three aspects of one process. Initially the process feels like it is all *here*. Immediately thereafter It seems like it is obviously coming from over *there*. Ultimately it announces Itself at one with *everywhere*.

The experience of alternately and then collectively being, Me, We and All - is part and parcel of everything that we create. What we see, touch, hear and feel inevitably reflects the unified state of our unified identity. The world we live in is the world we have created, willed into existence through our thoughts and actions - our choices staring at us as manifestations of our constantly evolving state of identity. Each point in the progression is fine unto itself. Yet pulling them all together - in zoom speed mind you - does take and depend on a special kind of knowingness.

Hmmm. Now that is a lot – at least for a little 'ol incarnate like you and me. But that is the gist of it - suggesting that we best stop shaking our heads in alleged confusion - and not only accept but affirm the fact that we create each facet of our ever evolving consciousness. Above all, we have every right to enjoy this incredible process and celebrate all our silly, and the sacred, and the wild and fascinating outcomes.

Modesty is a virtue but not if it is over extended and denies reality. Even the illusion of the so-called 'evil eye' can do little but imitate a frown on an otherwise high-spirited image. Nor can some crooked finger or invisible sword ever leave but a cursory mark. Even self-imposed doubts and momentary hesitations have little effect unless enlivened by some silly insecurity. We are who we are.

No false denial can disprove the simple truth: we are the children of The Divine, heirs to a sacred impulse, progenitors and bearers of a sacred lineage, creators of what is, has been and always will be. Our string of incarnate appearances can also progressively reveal the depth of Our involvement in divine process - which individually and collectively even enables us to discover the ineffable in the faces of our neighbors.

'Zow, and holy mackerel, and *that* just can't be' - is what we 'oft begin to say - fainting denial and scrunching our faces, making dismissive sounds and even displaying furrowed browses. Ultimately, however, we learn to embrace our experience and thereby affirm the presence of the sacred - in both our process and our personhood.

"We are indeed an integral portion of THAT' – a grand yet enormous slimming down of the infamous 'I am that I am", uttered by the Lord ITSelf to Moses as IT pronounced ITs presence in the Soul that was in the midst of attaining Its prophetic mission. [61] Our arms widen, our fingers reach out to their fullest extension, our breathing grows deeper and more complete, with any remaining hesitation being overwhelmed by affirmations of 'why not'... which soon gives way to 'could be' ... and is finally affirmed as, 'ah yes: it is so'.

Implications

If you agree – or are at least intrigued - then what are the practical implications of these truths? What can you do to heighten your awareness and give full expression to the fact that you are at depth an immortal Soul - although realizing as well that your prodigious identity is currently clothed in an awakened yet still vulnerable form of an everyday person?

Let's begin with the beginning.

1. The best way to start is to give thanks for being aware of your status as an immortal Soul, to affirm that you are an aspect or cell of the cosmic presence of The Lord. Your affirmation may be invoked with a full voice or murmured in relative silence. Either way it is best registered with a slight bowing of your head.

You may not receive an immediate pat on the back or news that your declaration is being applauded by society. But you may receive - later today, tomorrow or certainly soon - both a tangible sign and a knowing that your acknowledgement is received and deeply appreciated in Heaven.

2. Allow the objects in your home, room or office testify to your growing awareness of your soulful identity. What memories of spiritual encounters do your pictures and artifacts invoke? Spend a moment or two with those that best relive the original experience. You need not stay long

---

61 Exodus 3:14, also made abundantly clear in 6:3.

in reverie; it is simply important to keep those images alive as vivid reminders of the spiritual being you have always been and still are.

3. Amplify your ability to recall and reenergize the true highlights in your life - by turning off the telephone, putting your computer on simmer, allowing your mail to sit unattended - giving yourself the time and space to reconfirm how rich your life has been and how fortunate you are at this very moment.

4. Taking time to recall special memories. Honor those reconnections as they emerge - pausing for a moment to savor those that evoke a particular kind of happiness. Such spontaneous *allowing* will enable you to reaffirm your spiritual presence, update your sense of potential and remind you that you are indeed a very creative contributor to your own unfolding and that of your planet.

5. Get a large sheet of paper and draw whatever comes to mind - using scribbles, stick figures, lines and circles, whatever comes to mind. Be utterly spontaneous. Then make a list - using abbreviations or symbols - of all the things you already appreciate being or having.

Do another freelance drawing for all those things you still want to express or attract into your life.

Choose the top five items in each list. What do your matchings tell you? Do you see any patterns? Do the results make you laugh, cry, motivate to do something? If so, what if anything is preventing you from taking action and achieving what you want to do next?

6. Cultivate friends and associations that value what you value, including those who are already doing what you now wish to do. Order books and drawings that encourage you, that invite you to take a risk, go the next step, enable you to reach for and attain a level of happiness you earlier may have deemed impossible or silly.

7. Pass your best energies unto to others, wishing the best for any and all you meet. You might even do some little thing to help them on their way. For example, when moving about and completing a set of errands, be aware of anyone your intuition tells would appreciate a boost

or kind word, some extra energy, perhaps a healing, anything that brings them good fortune.

With a simple smile, perhaps a word or two, and an unobtrusive nod you can send the next passerby the kind of energy you intuitively think they will appreciate. As noted earlier, you could even raise your hand slightly - and unobtrusively - as you pass them and 'innocently' send them your blessings. Your intention alone can work wonders although an innocent wave of your hand or a gentle nod will insure delivery.

8. You can also send someone a prayer in the same way. Many of the walking wounded do not have bandaged heads or need a wheel chair. Their troubles are hidden but may still be real: not all losses and worries are displayed outwardly but may be buried beneath the façade of relative ease or just a furrowed brow. Either way, follow with your intuition and your keen eye. Mentally send people the energy you sense they need or could use - including a dose of pure energy to be used any way they choose.

9. Of course you always have the option to invoke more visible and tangible signs of your love by sending a friend or loved one a quick e-mail, postal card or a bouquet of flowers – on a special occasion or just because you want to let them know you are thinking of them and wishing them well.

10. When you next re-enter your home or office, be mindful of the pictures and objects you have selected. Attend especially to the tried and true members of your family and friends – especially those you may not have seen in a while.

Note the featured symbols or mementos, especially those that still resonate, that affirm your values – that remind you of your identity, your role, your rich heritage and your pledge to keep on 'keeping on'.

11. Now, go back to # 4, above: your drawings and the lists of what you love, need or want. It's time to make a plan on how you will attain those delights and put them on an approximate timetable. Review the plan within a day or two, adding to it or modifying it as you wish. Then - today - take at least some of the steps you outlined on your time table.

Attending and Creating

It is essential that you consistently image what you want to achieve or attain, then being sure to take the steps needed to create the kind of world you wish to live in. Maintaining focus and continuity in a world of enticing distractions is no easy task. In fact, it takes fortitude and commitment to actually attain anything you truly desire. This is especially true for attaining spiritual goals in any realm of life especially is the environment may be bland if not antagonistic.

Of course, many aspects of your business, family affairs and social life are likely to unfold as normal – and will need to be attended to as needed. The key is not to allow yourself to get overextended in any aspect of your life such that you neglect to cultivate your new and upgraded goals - especially if any of those goals involve a spiritual aspect.

'First things first', as they say, to be heeded not as a throwaway motto but as a day-to-day commitment. In fact, dealing with the details of life while staying true to what is central to your spiritual life is *the* essential task. It is indeed best to view everything through your spiritual lens. Lead with your soulfulness and everything will fall into line.

Such dedication does not justify your becoming a handy-dandy preacher who uses any excuse to turn every situation into a so-called spiritual encounter that gives you the right to comment on any offense allegedly committed by others. Rather pass no judgement and simply be a model for the behavior you prefer. And if you would be prayerful, invoke the advice of Joseph Campbell - and 'to do so in private'.

Wear any amulet that symbolizes who you are - including whatever logos you want on your t-shirts. Boldly display the pictures and affirmations that reflect your sense of values and purpose. Speak your truth when asked. But don't beat others over the head with any of it and try to become the conscience of your household or neighborhood. The spirit of love and understanding can best pervade a room - or a relationship - when we treat every situation and person we meet with dignity and compassion.

Besides, the world best responds to those who allow their actions to speak for themselves. Lecturing others on what they should say or do is a sign that puffery and pride may still be preferred over humility and love.

So be classy about your spiritual identity: outwardly humble, ever loving and attentive - yet inwardly at ease, confident, committed, just doing what you do best, just being the loving Soul that you are.

Re-Affirming Our Ancient Paradigm

It is indeed time that we reaffirm an ancient paradigm. We are all incarnates or embodiments of an immortal Soul. By inviting our Souls into our corporeal bodies – We, as a united being - are able to fulfill Our promise to further spiritualize the Earth as we normally move about the physical domain.

Thus I, Aeneas, an immoral Soul am the designated guide for William - who is My current incarnate or embodiment. Thus William is the official narrator of this book, although I continue to guide his decisions as I fulfill My role to act as the adhesive element - something like the intercellular gluon, [62] - that binds any related substances - like William, the Divine and I - together as one reality. No matter how varied My earlier 20,000 appearances, I have allowed each to operate with total free will, enabling them to follow, modify or reject any of the promises they made while preparing to incarnate.

Free will has always enabled My incarnates to choose how and where to live - thereby enabling them to experience and learn from as much of the cosmic expanse as possible. Such has been the continuing drama of My life in both the heavenly and the physical realms: aligned in intent, expanding

---

62 Gluon is the informal name used in sub-atomic physicists to describe the force that enables a quark - a set of elementary particles - that help to unify the elements of a cell - such as protons, neutrons and mesons - and bind them together.

as My composite skills allowed, and hard-wired to learn how to enshrine the priorities of Heaven on Earth.

Unity

Thus I, Aeneas, having invoked the energies of incarnation - have with Divine consent enabled each of my long line of incarnates to master the challenges We faced as We learned how to speak and act with unconditional love and compassion. As Prime Source and the Master Soul of Yeshua-Mary are One, so am I and My many incarnates also a unity and act as one. As Prime Source and the Master Soul are respectively transcendent to and immanent in the world, so is My immortal Soul capable of appearing as an incarnate in the world of everyday living.

To complete the spiritual connections: as I, Aeneas, am an aspect of The Lord, and I and My incarnates are as one, so are all the people who have ever incarnated in the physical realm embodiments of an immortal Soul and thus aspects of that which is inherently sacred. Those who throughout history declared that they were 'God' were actually evoking something essential although very much exaggerated: We incarnates who walk the Earth are indeed exalted in heritage for we reflect our Souls which are integral portions of God.

In this re-emerging paradigm or perspective, we all here on Earth are best likened to an *eidolon,* the term used in ancient Greek literature to indicate a spirit-image, a twin or look-alike. The poet, Walt Whitman, later used the term to indicate what he called the *oversoul,* the presence of an overseer or guiding Soul present within each person. We are each an integration of this 'two-in-one' combo, yet appear as 'one albeit *layered* being'. Each and every heavenly Soul is doing Its best to guide It's sets of incarnates or human expressions to think and act in ways that spiritualize the material realm.

Such truths lead Us to conclude that We are even more than an amalgam of immortal Soul and Our string of temporary incarnates. We are really - or also - 'three-in-One' manifestations of The Lord ITSelf. When many Christian churches annually celebrate 'All Souls Day', they unknowing are celebrating 'The Sacred Trio' of body, soul and spirit – not three separate entities present in the 'there after' but unified in the 'here-the now and forever-after'.

Fish need and thrive in water – yet apparently only realize that water is their essential environment when deprived of it. It is similar but in reverse with We inspired Souls and humanized embodiments: We may not realize it but We immortal Souls are able to thrive everywhere We go – in the ether world of heaven with The Lord, and with Earth's supply of oxygen when embodied as an incarnate. Wherever We are - We never cease to be. In fact, we are meant to thrive in either or both.

Restoring the Insights of the Originals

It is no surprise then, that the traditional reliance on organized religion is crumbling, that formalized institutions and their creeds are - for many - no longer considered the best repositories of spiritual energy.

The leaders of such structured religions as Catholicism, Judaism and Protestantism – as well as those charged with sustaining many of the formalized aspects of Hinduism, Shintoism and Buddhism – are well aware of the pressures to reform and loosen their infatuation with their ancient structures. Yet given their substantial power, many of their leaders resist dealing with those in their midst who have been calling for something less codified, stratified, defined and overtly if not inferentially judgmental.

The term *Spirituality* is admittedly vague for it is the generic energy of honoring the Sacred - and its reflection in the earthly practice of love and compassion. As such Spirituality supersedes the age-old propensity to erect the classifications, hierarchies and structures needed to sustain them. Rather, it vibrates best to the essence of The Lord and ITs unbounded creativity and love. Organized attempts to confine such eternal divine presence within the bounds of denominational codes only limits their force, attractiveness and effectiveness. Rather, the emphasis on the free flowing nature of 'spirit' honors the primary, universal and inclusive nature of the One - versus the defining and thus confining boundaries of the many.

Being In-Between

As the popularity and relevance of the formalized religions continue to fade, the openness of spirituality continues to gain in force. Any of the presently highly defined pathways to God will surely continue to be preferred and idolized by their most devoted followers - and so be it if it continues to meet their needs. But to the young and generalized public, however, many of today's formalized religions are in the process of following the demise of their predecessors. Their preference for some mixture of heavily defined proceedings, catechisms, structures, judgments and polarized assessments are increasingly considered irrelevant. Many are also finding themselves jousted on their own critical petards.

Simplicity is increasingly preferred over-elaborate construction, allowance over restricted boundaries, love over judgment, forgiveness over evaluation, and regard for individuality and diversity over mandates of standardization imposed by ecclesiastic authorities.

Openness, freedom and allowance are again the emerging needs of the day. Yet many sense the future but understandably hesitate. The act of relinquishing one's religion and then mustering the confidence to flow freely into an undefined future, can be highly disconcerting. Getting from the known *this and here!* to the amorphous *what and where?* can rightfully be experienced as moving into a state of *chaos. It is the sense of living in limbo, having surrendered what was allegedly known yet no new mooring has yet to appear.* [63] A friend refers to it perfectly as the *nullplace.* [64]

---

63 William F. Sturner, Risking Change (Buffalo, NY: Bearly Limited, 1987).
64 Conversation with Joyce Scozza Lubutti of Scarsdale, New York, September 1, 2020.

Offerings of Spirituality

If anything, the advocates and practitioners of spirituality do not wish to crown a new victor or quickly embrace a new format however flexible and individualized. Finding one's way to a new open-ended approach with no given side-rails takes time. Besides, becoming a party of one yet united in love and sentiment with kinsmen, friendships and close affiliations - is often what is preferred. But finding or attracting such a network of empathic souls can be very difficult, initially leaving you feeling very much alone if not lonely. Affirmation of and a deep trust in oneself then becomes essential - for the essence of your being knows you are onto something sacred. Tolerance for ambiguity becomes essential for it means you are finally relinquishing your dependence on and search for instant camaraderie, established pathways and ready-made answers.

Natural affinities for selected sources - including the wisdom communicated in some books, practices and traditions - do continue to emerge, and serve to reinforce an appreciation of just being alive - able to reach out to those who have at least some empathy and even connecting with some nice folks despite differences in belief and practice.

Those who honor a sense of deep spiritual underpinning without formal affiliations often tend to be more 'liberal', that is more accepting of deviations from what others may consider society's immoveable norms. Be who you wish, love who you wish, espouse what you what and live as you desire - leads to celebrating a sense of godliness wherever it appears. Any and everything is fine as long it is motivated by love and is committed to participating in the joys of compassion.

Trust As Energy and Essence

The spiritual way is thus a broader way, one that also offers a deeper perspective. Yet it is instinctively shunned by those who place a premium on winning vs. accepting, pride over equality, me-ism versus 'us', greed over integrity, outer success versus sacrificing for the common good, taking and accumulating versus giving, power over service, a 'one and only' approach versus the awareness that there are a million and one paths around, up and into the heart of the mountain.

A spiritually inspired end puts its emphasis on meaning rather than achieving, significance over accumulation, a way of life that seeks abundance for all rather than wealth and affluence for the few. As one of my spiritual colleagues puts it: "The New Earth is about caring for people, caring for the Earth and fulfilling our mutual responsibility to guard and protect the planet." [65]

Now the kicker: No matter how bad it gets, say the champions of this renewed call for the natural, direct and free way of honoring of God, everything that now exists really is absolutely okay. Such acceptance of the old while representing the new (which really is the ancient way) seems perfectly fine for mutual acceptance represents one more step in the great unfolding of a divine plan. In other words: 'Don't push the river: It flows all itself'! [66]

Amidst the occasional bouts of chaos, despite the publicized incidents that display the ups and downs of individuals and even entire societies, the intentions of the Divine are apparently ever present. [67] Despite the failings of the highly structured approaches to religion and our exasperation with it, there is something about the silly status quo is that is it exists within the context of Divine presence - and therefore seemed to be part of a divine plan and blessing.

Each situation - static conditions, status quo, new options, even revolution - may each receive the accepting or willful nod of divine will - each development shining through as needed - perhaps as the preface to the next and the next unfolding, assuring us that everything - despite all the disruptions and apparent setbacks and hanging on - are temporary steps

---

65 Joyce Scozza Lubutti, Scarsdale, New York, E-Mail dated September 3, 2020.

66 The title of a book by Barry Stevens (Celestial Arts Publishing, 1953).

67 See Frances Thompson, *The Hound of Heaven* (CreateSpace, 2016).

in the evolutionary advance of unfolding enlightenment. Such stories of yours and mine, like those of Yeshua and Mary, really are but metaphors, examples of where the flow of the divine now exists which contain hints - or assurances - of where it is heading. The arc of divinity presence and intent truly is being expressed by and within history. No established roadmap has been published but the direction of the divine and irresistible energy seems ever present.

To borrow from the old affirmation relating to one's personal health, 'each day and each year things are getting better and better'. Trust in the soulful nature of the universe is not only the energizer of our continued evolution. It is also the very essence of spiritual reality.

The Second Earth

There is another reason to trust in what appears to be an evolutionary thrust to the development of spirit in the earthly domain: we incarnate-Souls are in the midst of experiencing a wondrous upgrade in our living environment, namely the emergence of a 'new' or 'Second Earth'. The transit to this new spiritual and geographic home will involve a substantial expansion of our current level of consciousness. That long awaiting next step may very well be upon us.

In fact, We are already in the midst of the transition. Its pull is being felt by many as a demonstrable increase in spiritual awareness and understanding. It contains a clear invitation to all who are ready to transit from the fourth dimension to the fifth level of consciousness. The full transit will unfold in various ways for different people, each tug, sense or call to upgrade, to expand by going deeper - each one leading to the next, and the next level of appreciation and involvement.

The Souls impacted already sense the lure of greater horizons. They may become especially ever more sensitive to their capacity to create love and be especially recoiled by any display of vanity, selfishness, aggression or the neglect of others. Insights into the 'emerging goodness of life' may also appear more frequently along with experience little things as gifts of the majestic. Spirit may also appear through a variety of symbolic expressions: the sound of fluttering birds or musical notes, the sight of bubbling water, the sight of people helping others and a deeply intuitive feeling that suggests the presence of 'heaven' - is increasingly here, there, everywhere.

Moving into the fifth or even the sixth level of consciousness may also be experienced as literal 'time-outs' in which one may lose track of time or feel momentarily transited to some other realm. Such 'callings' may increase in number over time, and may even involve an awareness that you are gradually entering into another realm.

Apparently, the transfer to the realm of Earth II originally was slated to occur sometime within the period, 2032-35. But the continued cumulative neglect of the Earth has caused that timetable to speed up - such that many enlightened Souls began having mental and even physical glimpses of Earth II during the early months of 2022 - followed gradually by a periodic sense of momentary transiting. The sense of a full mental-emotional and even physical transit to Earth II is now predicted to occur for many during the period of 2024-30. Some may also learn how to balance such a transition with also maintaining a presence on the original Mother Earth - which may give way to systematic interchange if indeed the fate of old Earth declines precipitously, and is need of the elevated counsel of Earth II.

It is now estimated that all who have - by intention and history - earned the right to transfer to Earth II's more enlightened environment - will do so by approximately 2040. In the meantime, as noted, they may periodically bi-locate and develop a sort of 'dual citizenship' - alternating their sense of mental-emotional attachment and their actual physical 'residence' between the original Mother Earth and residence on Earth II as they wish and as conditions warrant. They will also be empowered to handle any issues that arise in their own transitions as they also assist others in making whatever type or degree of transition is right for them.

Unfortunately, the current Earth I will continue to be the home for all those who have consistently acted and voted to neglect the planet, or have based their lives on selfish materialism and the hatred of those they consider 'the other'. These are the folks who will face the consequences of their (in)actions and thus continue to live a-midst the planets' ongoing deterioration.

Those who choose and/or are selected to leave the old for the new will herald in a new model of citizenry. Such enhanced and highly soulful incarnates will likely to bear children who also volunteer, in turn, to sanctify other planets and settlements throughout the cosmos.

Assagioli and Pure Consciousness

The Italian psychologist, Roberto Assagioli, wrote several books – years ago – to set forth his psychology of *Psycho-Synthesis*. The essence of his studies and clinical practice was summed up in the power he ascribed to the will, the constructive guiding force that guides us to seek, embrace and trust what Assagioli referred to as 'the self'.

The process is clear and direct and thus can be encapsulated in a few declarations.

First, Assagioli declares the profound difference between our ego and our consciousness. The process involves the dis-identification of our everyday personal sense of ourselves in favor of an affirmation of our deeper and ever-lasting sense of consciousness. [68]

According to Assagioli, the awareness that transforms our everyday sense of identity into a realization of our true psychological or spiritual reality is summarized in the assertion: 'I recognize and affirm that I am a center of pure self-consciousness." [69]

He then urges us to affirm the following truisms:

"I have a body, but I am not my body."

---

68 This, of course, sounds like the spiritual difference between our embodiment and our immortal Soul. It also reflects the distinction psychologist Carl Jung makes between our sense of being an individual ego who is also empowered to access the energies and archetypes of the collective unconscious.

69 Roberto Assagioli, *The Act of the Will* (New York: Penguin/Viking/Esalen, 1973).

"I have emotions, but I am not my emotions."

"I have a mind, but I am not my mind."

"I have desires, but I am not my desires."

Rather, says Assagioli, he strongly asserts that all of us have the right to affirm the following affirmation: "I recognize and affirm myself as a center of pure self-awareness and creative, dynamic energy."

Each of us therefore has the right to declare that I can "at will – and at any moment – dis-identify from any (allegedly) overpowering emotion, thought [or] role", become "a detached observer of my own behavior and immediately re-establish the fact that I am not any of them. I am self-identified, not only the actor, but the director of my actions."

Assagioli thus invokes the power of the will to affirm oneself as the self-directed bearer of "pure consciousness". It is an affirmation that matches the power we earthlings have to affirm ourselves to be immortal Souls and thus aspects of the divine. Rather than merely serving for a while as a citizen of a tiny blue planet located somewhere at the edge of one arm of one of a million galaxies, we immortal Souls are integral facets of - and contributors to - IT All. We are, by Our divine identity, integral to God's perennial urge to love and continually *recreate* - ourselves, our immediate environment and our universe.

About the Narrator

William Francis Sturner, Ph.D. - known herein as the current incarnate of the immortal Soul, Aeneas - is the author of fifteen books, father of two children, playmate of six grandchildren, lover of art and music, psychotherapist and a very spirited and joyful presenter and facilitator.

Raised as a Roman Catholic, he gradually investigated other religious perspectives before devoting himself to the study of the mystical traditions and the practice of universal spirituality.

His work combines the perspective of growing up in the Bronx with the study and experience of Jungian, Gestalt and spiritual psychologies. His university appointments have included professorships at four American universities (Oakland, SUNY College-Buffalo, Massachusetts and Maine) and vice presidencies at two (Oakland and Buffalo State). He has also been awarded visiting appointments at the universities of Limerick, Ireland; Istanbul Technical, Turkey; Santiago de Compostela, Spain; and Moscow University, Russia.

His degrees include a B.S.S. from Fordham University (1957), a Masters in Communications from the University of Wisconsin (1960), a Ph.D. in Political and Organizational Studies at Fordham University (1965), and a Post Doctoral Certificate in Gestalt Psychology from the Gestalt Institute of Cleveland (1973).

Sturner's training includes forty years of studies in Jungian Depth Psychology with such centers as the Jungian Center in Kusnacht,

Switzerland; the New York Institute in Jungian Studies; and International Studies in Jungian Psychology (NH and VT).

He founded the 'Open Heart Sanctuary' in 2002 in East Aurora, NY, and has since moved it to the Sarasota-Nokomis area of Florida (2021). He now devotes his energies to communing with nature, investigating ancient and modern mystical traditions, and writing books that express the love and compassion of Universal Spirituality (US).

His earliest books on leadership, organizational development and creativity have over the years given way to volumes on mythic tales, a Jungian interpretation of creation, and the spiritual traditions of reincarnation. His most recent books have also focused on the various themes of spirituality, the continuing contributions of the Master Souls - Yeshua and Mother Mary - and now, with this volume, the interplay between the personal Me, Our immortal Soul, and Prime Source.